VICTORIA

Born in 1924, Weston Bate is Australia's leading local and regional historian. Educated at Scotch College, Melbourne, and the University of Melbourne, he served with the RAAF in World War II, taught at Brighton Grammar, Melbourne Grammar and the University of Melbourne. In 1978 he was appointed foundation Professor of Australian Studies at Deakin University. His publications include *A History of Brighton* and *Lucky City* (Ballarat 1851–1901); he is currently preparing a history of Ballarat since 1901.

Professor Boris Schedvin, series editor, teaches economic history at the University of Melbourne and is official historian of the Reserve Bank of Australia.

Originally published as part of a series entitled
Themes in Economic and Social History.
Edited by Professor Boris Schedvin, in association with the
Economic History Society of Australia and New Zealand.

Some Other Titles in the Series

R. V. Jackson, *The Population History of Australia*
Alan L. Lougheed, *Australia and the World Economy*
Tony Dingle, *Aboriginal Economy*

VICTORIAN GOLD RUSHES

WESTON BATE

The Sovereign Hill Museums Association

First published by McPhee Gribble Publishers
in association with Penguin Books Australia, 1988
Copyright © Professor Weston Bate, 1988
Copyright in the series
© C. B. Schedvin, 1988

Second edition published 1999 by
The Sovereign Hill Museums Association
Sovereign Hill Post Office
Ballarat, Victoria, Australia 3350
Telephone (03) 5331 1944
Facsimile (03) 5331 1528

National Library of Australia
Cataloguing-in-Publication data
Bate, Weston, 1924- .
Victorian gold rushes.
Bibliography.
Includes index.
ISBN 0 909874 20 4
1. Gold mines and mining – Victoria – History.
2. Victoria – History – 1851-1891.
3. Victoria – Social conditions – 1851-1891.
I. Title. (Series: Themes in Australian economic and social history).

994.503'1

CONTENTS

List of Tables

Map of Victorian Gold Towns, 1871
55

FOREWORD

Over the past thirty years the writing of Australian economic and social history has been transformed, and a substantial body of literature is available. Research in the field of economic history has become technical and draws on a large body of quantitative data. Writing in social history has also been adopting the methods of the social sciences, and the field now occupies a central place in Australian historiography.

The series will present important new information in an accessible and attractive form. The results of recent research will be drawn together, and fresh interpretations offered when appropriate. Students, teachers and general readers will find the series of particular value.

Each book will focus on a major aspect of our economic and social development. Authors are highly qualified, and topics have been especially selected in association with the Economic History Society of Australia and New Zealand. An essential part of each book will be a referencing back to original research, and a select bibliography.

Professor Weston Bate is an authority on Australian urban history, and author of a history of Ballarat in the nineteenth century. In this book he links economic, demographic, social and political issues in a lively fresh interpretation. He also explains how the gold rushes of the 1850s imparted a distinctive flavour to Victorian economic and social life.

C. B. Schedvin
Editor

INTRODUCTION

The lure and power of gold is conveyed throughout the centuries in legends like those about King Midas, Jason's quest for the golden fleece, Inca treasure and the Spanish Main. This rare, heavy, lustrous metal helped to transform the Australian colonies in the latter half of the nineteenth century, during what were also legendary times. For about ten years from 1849 in California, and from 1851 in Victoria, alluvial gold deposits attracted migrations of people on a scale unheard of in world history. By then economic and social tides flowing in Europe had swept away barriers that in earlier centuries had restricted gold seeking. Following the American and French revolutions of the late eighteenth century, democracy was on the march. It was possible, as never before, for ordinary people to join the search for the precious metal. Because Europe's deposits had been exhausted for centuries, that search would take them on long journeys overseas on ships that were larger, more numerous and more reliable than ever before.

But why gold? To answer that question it is necessary to understand the strength of capitalism in the dynamic commercial, industrial and colonial expansion of Europe at that time. Economic and population growth fuelled an explosion of activity. World trade, and therefore the demand for gold, its monetary lubricator, grew impressively, while new supplies of gold stimulated further

3

growth. There was a cumulative effect which Geoffrey Blainey explains.[1]

> In the 1850s Australia was so rich that its population demanded necessities and luxuries which her own industries could not yet provide. In the year 1853 Australia bought 15 per cent of the total value of goods exported from Great Britain, the world's largest exporter. Britain's exports to the new gold countries of North America and Australia increased by 271 per cent in the years 1846-53; and in the same period Britain's exports to the rest of the world increased by only 21 per cent. There is evidence that California and then Australia had such purchasing power that they largely revived the sick economy of Britain, which in turn sent a chain reaction of prosperity around much of the civilized world . . . For example, the voyage from Europe to the goldlands was so popular and so long that more ships were needed for the traffic, and ship-building yards in Boston and Glasgow and Tyneside prospered. The wages they paid revived trade in their own vicinity; the timber and hemp and iron they imported as raw materials spread prosperity to other industries and other countries like a chain letter.

Gold was the international standard of exchange. Although widely used, paper money was still regarded with suspicion. In an increasingly commercial world, gold was the most secure of assets. Once ordinary people and new communities were able to win it, gold became an engine of social change. How powerful is one of the most interesting questions in Australian history.

Of basic importance was the impact of gold on Australian demography. The precious metal attracted mostly young and vigorous migrants. In contrast to the convicts and government assisted migrants who had preceded them, those who came freely from Europe to Australia in the 1850s seem to have been equipped to play a very important part in commercial, industrial and agricultural development. At the same time the Chinese added a racial dimension that had been little noticed before in Australia because the Aborigines had been swept aside.

A useful framework for understanding the interaction of social and economic factors in the new society influenced by gold is the concept of cultural transmission. By that is meant the transfer to Australia of old world institutions and ideas as part of the life experience of the migrants. An unusual mix of people was deposited. They achieved a new planting (onto pastoral foundations) of the ideas, aspirations and institutions they found meaningful in their homelands. There was also, for Australia, a rare up-country-urban emphasis, and a mass experience not rivalled until World War I. Democratic ideas were reinforced by democratic social conditions. An interesting indication of this is that goldfield communities had easily the highest level of homeownership in the world.

As a premier asset, gold gave unusual power to local communities. It helped them to diversify investment far beyond mining, especially in Victoria, where fertile hinterlands provided many goldfield towns with economic opportunities and permanent populations of a size denied to their counterparts in New South Wales, California, South Africa and Western Australia. The presence of agricultural, pastoral and timber resources helped to keep down mining costs, just as mining provided hinterland settlers with ready markets. What economists describe as linkages (e.g. investment forward from wheat-growing to flour-milling for market and backward to manufacture of fertilizer) were established. Local industries received extra strength, early on, through the natural protection from outside competition given to goldfields communities by poor transport from the coast. By the time railways had been constructed to the Victorian goldfields in 1862, spectacular and diverse economic growth had occurred.

In assessing the nature and strength of the cultural transmission resulting from the goldrush, it is necessary to be clear about elements of the pre-gold society. What distinguished the Australian experience from the Californian was the relative strength and the centralized nature of Australian government. Australia's convict foundation contributed to that. Fear of ex-convicts led to a strong government presence on the goldfields, and concern to deter labourers from leaving their jobs in the pastoral industry prompted the introduction of a stiff licence fee for diggers. An official decision to allow only small claim sizes (in contrast to large Californian claims) also greatly influenced the way mining and mining society would develop.[2] Thus, the new arrivals were influenced by the previous phase in the creation of Australian society. In Victoria, expecially, the gold migrants received unsympathetic treatment. Their disadvantage was magnified by the stranglehold gained by pre-gold interests in the Legislative Council, the upper house of Parliament. Council members were able to thwart the goldfields democracy, and to hinder the later development of mining by defeating moves to legalize mining on private property.

The goldrush strongly influenced the distribution of population in Australia. New South Wales lost its early supremacy to Victoria and within Victoria the pre-gold concentration on the port-capital of Melbourne was weakened. During the 1850s Melbourne's proportion of Victoria's population fell from 38 to 23 per cent. It was not until the 1880s that Melbourne's merchants and manufacturers regained their earlier dominance.

From the emphasis already given to Victoria, it should be apparent that Australian deposits were unequally distributed. If those of Coolgardie and Kalgoorlie discovered in the 1890s had been located near the south-west coast and exploited earlier, Australian history would have been quite different. Even so, surface alluvial deposits, which gave such benefit socially to Victoria, were weak in Western Australia. It should be stressed that gold deposited people in accordance with the time of discovery and the geology of individual fields. The sequence of discovery and exploitation, anti-clockwise, around the continent is a special theme of Geoffrey Blainey's *The Rush That Never Ended*. He once remarked amusingly that gold was usually found near pubs and then, seriously, that the pastoral expansion was a prospecting spearhead. Shepherds often found gold, and there was much less chance for finds to be made in remote and desert areas. The more pleasant and populated areas like Victoria were quickly explored.

The history of each goldfield fitted into a general sequence. The rich surface alluvials exploited in 1852 and 1853 at Castlemaine and Bendigo in Victoria were like a trial run. New fields after that were tackled more confidently and with almost instantaneous urbanization. Similarly the buried streams of Ballarat and Creswick, on which deep mining was pioneered in 1853 and 1854, can be seen as the training ground for the exploitation of similar deposits in northern Victoria and New Zealand to which capital and expertise were exported from Ballarat. The wave which swept north, then west and south around Australia broke quickly each time new deposits were discovered. A short alluvial crest with the turmoil of surface digging was followed by a longer, underground, company phase. More and better machinery became available from the original large centres where schools of mines trained geologists, managers, engine-drivers and other experts. Their early primacy gave places like Ballarat and Bendigo a continuing influence and ensured the supremacy of Victorian capital in gold mining; until the 1890s depression, that is, when Melbourne floundered and lacked the substance to profit from the peak Western Australian discoveries.

An even larger movement than that within Australia is evident in links with California. Over 6,000 Australians went to California in a few years after 1849 and many brought back skills and equipment like the cradle from 'placer' (alluvial) fields. They were joined by the tribe, drawn from all nations, who had journeyed half across the world to San Francisco and now continued to follow the gold trail across the Pacific. Their attitudes came too and, when California met a downturn from 1852, so did the produce of Boston, New York and other cities on the eastern seaboard of the United States, which were already geared up to supply excellent goods for pioneer outposts. Clipper ships, of the last and greatest era of sail, were diverted to the Australian trade and many thousands of Chinese, prompted by declining returns in California, were redirected in a well-organized scheme to the 'new gold mountain'. Because of its place, therefore, in the sequence of discovery, Australia received a strong injection of American experience. American influence on what was soon to be regarded as the most Yankee of British colonies will be seen in the story of Victoria.

AN ECONOMY TRANSFORMED

General Impact

The discovery of gold in Victoria had major effects on the Australian economy. The first and most obvious was on the size of the system. The population of the Australian colonies more than doubled from 405,356 in 1850 to 1,168,000 in 1861. There were also structural changes. Gold replaced wool as the leading sector of the economy for almost twenty years.[3] At the same time the focus of economic activity moved from New South Wales to Victoria. What had been in 1851 a small settlement of 77,345 people on the pastoral frontier of the mother colony had grown to 540,322 in 1861. The price of labour increased dramatically. All non-goldfields activity had to contend with severe labour shortages which in the long-term stimulated technological change in the pastoral industry and promoted the mechanization of agriculture.

The Australian financial system matured rapidly. The exploitation of gold deposits greatly increased money income and stimulated the formation of new banks.[4]

The domestic saving rate was lifted dramatically, which for some time reduced dependence on overseas borrowing. This enabled the banks to accumulate financial assets in the United Kingdom and encouraged further British investment in Australia.

In the overall pattern of Australian economic development the goldrushes were important for consolidating the primacy of the south-east of the continent. They raised Melbourne to equal status with Sydney and started its long reign as the financial capital of the nation. They stimulated the industrialization of Victoria, enabling that colony to share with New South Wales the capacity to take strong advantage of further industrialization during the world wars of the twentieth century. Gold also influenced the spread of the pastoral industry by speeding up its development in Victoria's Western District whence the younger sons of established grazing families moved to new opportunities, first in the Riverina and then in western New South Wales and outback Queensland. The contribution of the Victorian fields to the New South Wales pastoral industry, both as a market for meat and as a source of labour,[5] is just one facet of inter-colonial activity. The vast inland corridor, west and north of the Great Dividing Range, carried a heavy traffic in animals, produce and people.

Economic historian N. G. Butlin in estimating the value of gold production in comparision with that of wool (Table 1) has joined a

Table 1

Shares in Australian Gross Domestic Product, 1850–65

per cent

	Mining	Pastoral	Non-Pastoral Primary
1850	2.8	15.2	19.4
1851	5.2	15.4	18.9
1852	36.4	7.8	7.8
1853	27.9	8.9	6.9
1854	18.8	9.4	7.6
1855	21.7	8.3	13.3
1856	23.3	9.1	13.5
1857	21.7	9.1	11.8
1858	19.5	9.8	13.3
1859	18.0	10.2	13.3
1860	16.7	10.2	13.5
1861	15.7	7.8	12.8
1862	15.2	8.6	13.3
1863	14.3	7.5	14.1
1864	13.1	11.4	12.6
1865	12.8	9.5	13.7

Source: N. G. Butlin (1986).

long debate about the relative importance of the goldrush in Australian history. In the narrow sense these findings are decisive: gold was dominant in the mid-1850s but then its relative importance declined swiftly. Economic historians have also argued that the linkages backwards and forwards from gold were weaker than those from, say, wheat where flour milling (forward) and agricultural machinery production (backward) added strength to the economy. Figures are not available to measure this influence but the comparison with gold can be discussed in general terms. Whilst forward linkages from gold were weak – some coins were minted in Australia – there is evidence that backward linkages were strong. The creation of towns alone was a significant economic outcome.

Mining required labour, equipment and supplies on a scale far above the needs of the pastoral and agricultural sectors. The deeper workings of the 1860s absorbed an immense supply of timber for head works, shafts and drives and as firewood to fuel boilers. Those boilers, together with engines, quartz-crushers, pumps, pipes and haulage gear (which also needed constant repair) provided work for many foundries and machine shops. Miners' clothing and equipment, their high protein food and housing needs, stimulated primary and secondary industry to a degree not experienced in pastoralism and agriculture. The lure of gold kept companies working on marginal claims and, because overseas interest commitments were small in an industry largely financed locally, the gains were largely ploughed back into the Australian economy.

Geological Influences

Beneath these general patterns of growth lay the uncertainties surrounding gold discovery. Even when found, deposits could be difficult to exploit. Some required quite sophisticated financial and mechanical operations. The geology of goldfields must therefore be understood before their economic importance can be assessed.

The nature and the location of fields had a large bearing on the economic life of their communities. In Blainey's and Serle's general accounts, as well as in numerous studies of particular goldfields, it is evident that surface alluvial deposits were the only sites where masses of diggers were found. This ensured that the first alluvial phase, however rich, was frantic and short lived. Without deeper gold, lasting settlement, although it did occur, was unlikely. Deeper deposits, whether in quartz reefs or buried streams, required specialist financial, mining and sometimes metallurgical skills. The timing of finds was also important. Bendigo's reefs, for instance, gave steady returns for decades, but a gap between the alluvial and the quartz phases on that field ensured that to exploit the quartz outside capital had to be brought in. This led to the ownership of mines by individual capitalists. In contrast, the Ballarat field had been buried as a result of the lava flows that covered Victoria's Western District. Ballarat was therefore more complex than Bendigo and had little surface gold. It was plagued by underground water, but experienced an unusual continuity of investment, mainly through local capital organized in co-operative companies. That continuity resulted from an early involvement in deep sinking (requiring capital and organization), which was necessary as miners followed underground the various stream deposits they had originally discovered near the surface.

Even at the alluvial stage there were important differences, mainly related to the availability of water. Mountain fields like Beechworth in Victoria and Kiandra in New South Wales could use the 'long tom' and other sluicing techniques developed in California to wash out the gold with a continuous flow of water. At drier Bendigo, where shortage of water was always a problem [6] and where sticky clays were dominant, an Australian technique of 'puddling' was adopted. At first the gold bearing clays were mixed with water in an old provisions tub and broken up by spade. Later they were scoured by farmers' harrows in the circular troughs of horse-driven puddling machines. Ballarat was unique because in its buried landscape the original streams had to be followed at depth through very wet ground. The water situation was reversed; it had to be baled (and later pumped) continuously to get to the gold. In northern and western Australian, in the absence of water, 'dry-blowing' was used to separate the gold from the earth. When thrown into the air the lighter particles blew away, leaving the heavy gold to fall straight down. Precious water had to be saved to preserve life.

Mineral Economy

Discovered first because of their location in settled pastoral areas, the Victorian fields, through their wealth, proximity to ports, fertile hinterlands and temperate climate, were the pump-primers of the Australian mineral economy. Famous not only for quantity of gold, but also for a wide band of country in which nuggets of unusual size were found[7] they drew to Australia an unusual group of migrants through whose efforts a much stronger and more diversified economy was built.

An important engine of economic growth was gold itself, but its nature has to be better understood if we are to appreciate what that meant. For millions of years nature had broken up the quartz reefs and deposited pure gold in streams and terraces. Internationally it had been given special status as currency, so that anyone who found it could be sure of receiving close to its official value from banks and gold buyers. What was most needed on the great alluvial fields was toughness, determination and luck. In that way, as observers constantly remarked, gold was a great leveller. This meant that the profits from digging were spread widely. No third party, such as a processor or sales agent, could get between the digger and his winnings. And unlike wool, grain and other commodities, the price of gold was remarkably stable. Moreover, because the cost of transporting it was small, a very large share of its value went to those who produced it.

The fact that gold was a prime financial asset benefited communities as well as individuals. Their winnings were ploughed back into further mining and used in general development. This gave inland communities an unusual opportunity. In the centralized Australian banking and financial system, dominated, as John McCarty[8] has pointed out, by the commercial capital cities, there was otherwise little possibility of up-country urban development. Before gold was discovered, merchants sat like spiders at the centre of the pastoral web; afterwards, local financial systems, including stock exchanges at major goldfields, emerged to tap the immense wealth. Ballarat and Bendigo between them produced about 16 million ounces of gold between 1851 and 1870. Much of the profit was re-invested especially in small-scale ventures. Early on store-keepers 'grubstaked' miners, by taking shares in their claims in return for supplies. Successful miners began businesses or took up farms.[9] This strengthened local investment and expressed a tendency among individuals to defend their stake in their communities by providing capital for mining, urbanization and hinterland growth. The Ballarat Bank was a notable example of the general use of accumulated capital. Conscious of the importance of the hinterland to the town and aware of an excellent local market, it claimed that it had lent generously to farmers in the five years from 1865.[10] The Ballarat land agent, James Oddie, a pioneer digger, a self-improving Wesleyan and a democrat, personally loaned large amounts to Ballarat men seeking their future in agriculture. The Anderson brothers, whose large timber milling operations in the Bullarook Forest, north-east of Ballarat, were a backward linkage out of mining, diversified into agriculture and then (as a forward linkage) into flour milling, all on the strength of goldfields demand.

Legal factors influenced economic performance. The small claim size adopted by government regulation in New South Wales and copied in Victoria produced a tendency for frantic rushes and the rapid exploitation of surface deposits. This was quite unlike the situation in California where, as Blainey remarks,[11] large claims gave greater stability and less resistance to the introduction of capital.

Australian diggers were hostile to large-scale capitalist undertakings using wage labour. English investors expected the Colonial Office to secure special privileges for them, but only one company of consequence, among forty or so funded from Great Britain, was successful, and then only after several false starts. That was the Port Phillip Gold Mining Company, which eventually achieved profits from quartz on a freehold taken up at Clunes in 1857.[12] Local and small capitalists were outraged that the efforts and sacrifices people had made to migrate and dig for gold could be negated by armchair investors. Because of their protests, leasehold legislation of 1853, giving mining rights for five years to 160 acres of abandoned alluvial ground and a mile along quartz veins was never implemented. Small holdings remained the norm until the late 1850s by which time, because the best alluvials were exhausted, it was obvious that larger capital organization was needed. Importantly, this was achieved through a plough-back of profits from general economic development. Melbourne, as against goldfields (or British) investors, began to play an important role. There was a boom (some called it the 'mining revolution') in the formation of public companies.[13] But there was wild gambling and a serious failure to realize the need for long-term investment.

The extent of capital plough-back on different fields is of great importance in distinguishing between them. The steadiness, for different reasons, of Ballarat and Beechworth contrasts with a fractured experience at Bendigo, where a break between the rich surface alluvial and the machine puddling era was followed by a further interval between puddling and quartz. As a result, new capital from outside was needed for the expensive entry into quartz mining.[14] Eventually private ownership of mines became the norm, whereas at Ballarat co-operative deep-sinking in the buried streams of the alluvial basin led naturally to large co-operative companies working the same streams as they were followed deeper still under the basalt plateau. The local community retained financial control of the mines.

The contrast between Ballarat and Bendigo continued into the 1870s and 1880s, when problems with underground water and the uncertainties of the buried landscape made Ballarat less predictable than Bendigo, where the famous 'saddle reefs' lay neatly beneath each other. Many more short-lived, small companies were to be found at Ballarat. In another distinction, Bendigo's quartz was outstandingly rich, while Ballarat had massive formations which were very easy to work. From a similar volume of quartz in 1873, for instance, Bendigo produced nearly three times as much gold as Ballarat. And in 1880, to extract about the same amount of gold as Bendigo, Ballarat mines had to crush about twice as much stone.[15] Cusack[16] speaks of the excitement generated by Bendigo quartz.

Almost everywhere in Victoria, after 1860, capitalists were

dominant. Stock exchanges became as important as mining claims. Ballarat's 'Corner', where business was conducted in the open air at the corner of Lydiard and Sturt Streets, and Bendigo's 'Beehive', were clearing houses for shares and barometers of the state of mining. Stockbrokers exerted a large influence. Many were leading investors and promoters, with great wealth and social standing. Of course, mining investment like prospecting was a lottery. Chance could still bring a fortune. Yet there was a sense in which whole communities believed that investment in mines was an act of local patriotism.

Economic Instability

Risks as great as those in mining were taken by British (especially) manufacturers and merchants who sent goods to what seemed to be an insatiable market. They were often caught. There was a glut, for instance, in 1854, which added to the government's problem in managing the goldfields (see p. 42) and a very serious situation emerged in 1857 when English consignors again flooded the Victorian market with goods. Gold production fell but migrants kept arriving. In such a market economy the adjustment was painful. Although, as Butlin and Sinclair's figures indicate,[17] there was only a slight drop in Victoria's Gross Domestic Product during 1855 and a rapid recovery to 1853 levels, the trading instability was serious. The following passage from Serle's *The Golden Age*[18] discusses the problem:

> The years 1854 to 1861 were a time of rapid deflation. As imported goods were continually in a state of over-supply, as local primary produce became freely available and conditions of transport steadily improved, prices fell steadily to somewhere near the pre-gold level, while wages on the whole followed close behind, especially after unemployment became serious in 1857. The world slump of that year had very little effect on Victoria's well-insulated economy which rested primarily on local mining capital, and the price of gold remained unchanged. In its comparative independence of British capital until the railway loan, Victoria of the fifties is an exceptional case in Australian history. But it had cyclical problems enough of its own of which

the most important, perhaps, were the fluctuations in import-consignments which continually upset the market and had wide repercussions.

That behaviour bears out Blainey's comment that gold had significant effects on world trade. But the slow pace of communications meant that overseas shippers, merchants and manufacturers were often acting on inadequate information and from an over-optimistic view of the continuance of dazzling gold strikes. Immigration was influenced by the same optimism. Serle[19] explains that the unemployment crisis of 1857 was aggravated by a surprisingly large immigration from Great Britain. It was double that of 1856 and not far below the pace of the original rush of 1852-4. The Victorian government had compounded the problem by stepping up assisted migration. The goldfields could not absorb the flood, Melbourne was overcrowded and little land was available for settlement. The engine of development stalled and there was mass unemployment that produced strong political repercussions.

Diversification

Despite that crisis, Victoria had been able to consolidate the economic strength and population gains of the first half of the 1850s. By an enormous expansion of the overall economy, related in part to the fertile countryside, an increasingly large proportion of the immigrants had been absorbed into activities beyond mining. Ballarat may be taken as a case study. Early in 1854 one observer at Ballarat noticed that 'a great many tradesmen are returning to their trade, so at present large buildings are in course of erection'.[20] A year later he described Ballarat as a great place of business. By 1857 Main Street in the diggings was lined for two and a half kilometres by stores, hotels and workshops. There were over four hundred properties in all, carrying stock worth perhaps £1 million. The road from the port of Geelong, of which Main Street was the final leg, was crowded with huge wagons bringing in supplies. As part of a transport revolution, American Concord coaches, made famous by Cobb and Co., gave passengers a surprisingly quick and reliable service.[21]

Attention should be focused on the road to Geelong. Winter made it almost impassable for heavy traffic and cartage was costly at the best of times. In consequence, until the railway from Geelong was completed in 1862, local farming, manufacturing and timber-getting were stimulated. Timber, hay, potatoes, grain and other foodstuffs had to be carted only a fraction of the distance from the coast. The manufacture of candles, soap, boots, harness, agricultural implements and many other items was similarly boosted. Inland areas of population were thus given 'natural protection' from overseas, intercolonial and coastal competition. Candles and boots, with which miners were illuminated and shod, were backward linkages to the slaughter of animals for food. A metal fabricating industry grew from the need to keep machinery operating. Wet shafts required continuous pumping. Because spare parts had to be individually made and fitted in those days before mass production, and because long delays occurred if the work was sent to Geelong or Melbourne, foundries and machine shops emerged locally. Ballarat had two foundries in 1856. By 1860 there were ten, making most of the engines, pumps, quartz-crushers and hauling gear for the maturing mines. For smaller jobs large numbers of blacksmiths could be found.

Employment in the metal industry was small as a proportion of the total workforce but it was significant. Every goldfield needed many blacksmiths. Table 2 shows the number of metal workers on each goldfield in 1871. Proportionately Ballarat was the largest, followed by Castlemaine and Bendigo, but crude employment figures do not indicate relative sophistication. A more revealing set of figures, which appears in the statistics of Victoria for 1871 (Table 3), shows that in manufacturing as a whole Ballarat was not merely larger but much more sophisticated. Ballarat West, the site of most of the foundries, was very heavily capitalized. As quartz mining strengthened so did Bendigo's metal industry. Cusack[22] emphasizes its growth in the 1870s and 1880s when, at least in the manufacture of mining machinery, its foundries challenged the supremacy of Ballarat.

The technological experience of Ballarat manufacturers gave them an advantage during the expansion of company mining elsewhere in Australia. From 1862 the railway became the means by which their products were widely distributed. The manufacture of farm implements, culminating towards the end of the century in the famous Sunshine Harvester of H. V. McKay, was a natural backward linkage from grain production. The strongest agricultural areas of the colony were close to Ballarat in the late 1850s and were prosperous throughout the 1860s, after which the opening to the west of wheatgrowing on the blacksoil plains of the Wimmera and then the red Mallee sands confirmed Ballarat as a farm machinery manufacturing centre.

Table 2

Male Employees in the Metal Industry on the Victorian Goldfields, 1871

Ararat	Ballarat	Beechworth	Castlemaine	Maryborough	Sandhurst (Bendigo)
85	798	174	487	396	432

Source: Census of Victoria.

Table 3

Factories and Workshops in Selected Victorian Goldfields Municipalities, 1871.

Town	Number of Workshops	Horsepower	Hands Employed	Value of Machinery
Ballarat West	49	370	851	£258,648
Ballarat East	23	93	223	£8,840
Castlemaine	16	60	183	£23,890
Sandhurst (Bendigo)	29	152	384	£47,575

Source: Statistics of Victoria.

As Serle[23] comments, the area of cultivation in Victoria grew during the 1850s by about 60,000 acres a year, from 55,000 in 1854 to 419,000 in 1860. It was more than double the increase in the six succeeding years of the Selection Acts. He speculates that most of the 10,000 new farmers must have been diggers and goes on to explain the relationship of agriculture to the goldfields.

> The quickest expansion was near the goldfields. In the four gold counties of Ripon, Talbot, Dalhousie and Grenville alone, the number of holdings grew between 1856 and 1861 from some 560 to about 3,350, and cultivation to about one-third of the colony's. Here and round the old-established inland farming centres there was great prosperity . . .

'Proximity to markets' and natural protection by distance and cartage costs from imported grain were indeed the conditions of success before the railways opened up competition. Many of these farms had reapers and steam-threshing machinery whose use was sometimes objected to by labourers 'as an invasion of their rights'. The flour-mills also received natural protection and were thriving. You can see them across the countryside today, some still standing but many in ruins like old mines.

Serle goes on to describe the less prosperous farming scene near the coast where producers were exposed to competition from imported grain and flour. A farmer at Melton complained that grain could be shipped from Liverpool to Melbourne more cheaply than he could cart it the intervening forty kilometres. It is an important point. Because natural protection did not work for them, the coastal farmers became the spearhead of a campaign for tariff protection. Manufacturers naturally joined in.

Pastoralism Transformed

A book could be written about the effects of the goldrushes on pastoralism. Margaret Kiddle's *Men of Yesterday* (1961) explains how the profits made by pastoralists from goldfields markets helped them to find the funds needed to buy the freeholds of their Western District runs in the 1850s and 1860s. In his book *The Riverina* G. L. Buxton (1967) discusses the use of the river frontages of the Murray-Darling system to fatten and hold livestock for the Victorian market. Animals for this trade were bred further north and east on the slopes of the Great Dividing Range, as O. B. Williams explains in an interesting chapter in *The Simple Fleece*,[24] Susan Priestley, in *Echuca*[25] discusses the stock traffic from the vantage point of Echuca, 'the oesophagus of Victoria'. Geoffrey Blainey provides the useful thought that wool was a 'lame staple' in Australia before gold. Graziers then were at the mercy of fluctuations in the overseas price of wool. But with a vast new population they could profit from the broader domestic market for meat, hides and tallow. As Serle[26] says 'The huge new local market for meat was the squatter's greatest recompense for the invasion of his solitude.' Wool production rose and the glut of shipping brought export freight rates down. Victoria's cattle population doubled, despite high consumption, and the breeding of horses, as 'engines' for whims, puddling machines, drays and coaches, was very profitable.

Labour intensive activity in mining, building and the construction of roads and railways stimulated the production of food and the necessities of life. Because wages were high, even the unskilled enjoyed a material standard of living far better than they would have expected in the old world. As the *Ballarat Star* reported in 1871:

> Legs of mutton a shilling a couple, rabbits at the same price, butter, cheese and vegetables at very moderate rates, made the markets a place where the poorest purchasers could furnish forth such a Sunday feast as hundreds of thousands of honest working men in the old country can enjoy only in unrealisable dreams . . .[27]

The general wealth of the community also ensured that the demand for housing and goods like furniture, stoves and cooking utensils was strong.

Transport Revolution

Horses have often been overlooked in Australian history. They were central to a transport revolution in which slow moving bullocks were replaced by faster, more flexible animals. Much of the hay and oats, which occupied almost half the cultivated ground in Victoria in the 1850s, fuelled these hardworking tractors.[28] Breeding them became big business. As mentioned in *Lucky City*,[29] 'Draught horses were the centre of attention at local shows as taste followed profit into the haulage industry.' Semi-draughts, still strong, but faster, were used on the rapidly expanding coach routes, as carrying people became more and more important. Changed every fifteen or twenty kilometres, coach-horses kept up a spanking pace on rough roads, thanks to American engineering in light, leather-sprung Concord coaches and the energy of men like the American Freeman Cobb and his partners in Cobb and Co.

The main roads, especially at first, could not support cumbersome vehicles of the English tradition. Despite the expenditure of vast sums of government money, they remained graveyards for bogged and overturned wagons, which broke down in the struggle to keep the goldfields supplied. In the mid–1850s it cost £80 a ton to send goods one hundred kilometres to Ballarat from Geelong, ten times the price it was to cost by rail in the next decade. That high cost was, as has been mentioned, the basis of the natural protection by which industrial and agricultural production was stimulated up-country. Indicative of the adventurous attitudes of the time was an order placed by a syndicate of miners with Morgan, a Ballarat coach builder, for a coach to carry over 80 people.[30] When the syndicate failed, Cobb and Co. took over the monster, called it the Leviathan, put 'Cabbage-tree' Ned Devine on the box and placed it on the Geelong-Ballarat run. That vehicle may have represented a feeling of frustration with the limitations of contemporary road transport. But the huge capital cost of railways meant that no alternative was available for the Victorian goldfields before 1862 and in New South Wales before the 1870s. As a sign of the greater potential for coaches in the absence of railways, Cobb and Co. moved its headquarters to Bathurst, New South Wales, in 1862. That was the year when Melbourne was connected by rail to Bendigo (with an extension soon afterwards to the Murray River at Echuca) and Geelong to Ballarat.

With hindsight, it is clear that a Geelong-Melbourne line, sponsored by capitalists from Geelong and completed in 1857, with very large overseas borrowing, was a mistake.[31] The success of Australia's first railway, from Port Melbourne to the city, was not repeated because bay steamers were much cheaper and because the hope that Geelong would become the main colonial port was frustrated by the government's unwillingness to dredge a passage through a sand bar across Corio Bay. Geelong's boosters believed that Melbourne interests had defeated them, but they were dreaming. Although Geelong was 40 kilometres closer to Port Phillip Heads, the cost of rail transhipment would have been prohibitive.

Where Geelong might have gained an advantage was in trade with Ballarat. A better port and a connection by rail to that goldfield rather than Melbourne in the mid-1850s would have limited the need for a metal industry at Ballarat, thus locating foundries at Geelong; and by cutting natural protection for foodstuffs this situation might have given Geelong dealers a large share of the profits of the Ballarat market. But who was to know that the Ballarat mines would be so rich? Overseas investors would not have been prepared for such a gamble.

Without the goldrush, it is hard to believe that railways up-country would have been attempted for decades. They cost £135,000 a mile. Like the boom in public building they were the product of British thinking, being very solidly constructed. In the way Cobb and Co's light coaches made their heavy British counterparts obsolete, American-style light railways, according to Blainey,[32] would have changed the picture completely. They would not have imposed such a large financial burden on the colony.

Role of the State

Without a strong lead from government, railways might have been further delayed. They were a watershed in state participation in economic development. As Serle[33] explains they helped 'centralized paternalism . . . to become a habit', thus laying the foundations of the peculiarly Australian mixed economy, which N. G. Butlin has described as colonial socialism.[34] Serle quotes the commission on the civil service in 1859 as evidence of how far the matter had gone in Victoria in such a short time:

The Government of this country is compelled to conduct the business of a great landowner – to survey, to lease, and to sell its property, its town lots, its country lands, its pastures, and its mines; to construct and maintain roads and bridges, and other works of public utility; to form railways and electric telegraphs; to assist municipalities, road boards, mining boards, and charitable institutions; to establish and supervise lighthouses, lunatic asylums, pounds, and cemeteries, and to do many other acts which in older countries possessing similar institutions are effected either through private enterprise or through local exertion.[35]

The state assumed responsibility for the railways in three main steps. First the Victorian government guaranteed the interest repayments on loans raised in Britain by the first three railway companies.[36] Then it decided to undertake (albeit through contractors) the construction of the Geelong-Ballarat and Melbourne-Bendigo-Echuca lines, intending to let private enterprise operate them when completed. Finally, it took over the operations itself. There was security for overseas investors in government borrowing and a release of private capital for other purposes. On the labour side, also, government spending was of critical importance. In 1857, when alluvial mining was beginning a rapid decline, there were apparently about 3,000 former railway navvies in the colony. They were attracted to railway construction gangs which, in the depressed years that followed, provided effective unemployment relief.[37]

─────────────────── **Wider Effects** ───────────────────

As suggested earlier, the goldrush was a pump-primer for the mineral industry in general. The mobilization of local capital, the attraction of overseas investment, the immigration of expert miners and the development of geological and metallurgical skills all helped. When the search for gold located other ores, or when the mineral fever spread as it did to the Barrier Ranges and revealed the silver of Broken Hill in 1885, men trained at the Schools of Mines at Ballarat and Bendigo were in great demand.

Although goldmining technology was relatively simple, some difficult ores stimulated scientific experiment. General technical competence improved immensely in the 1860s and 1870s as the mines went deeper and adopted the latest approaches to pumping, drilling and explosives. Easily set dynamite made blasting powder redundant. As well as improving ventilation, compressed air replaced hand-hammered drills underground, while, by the 1880s, steam-driven drilling rigs on the surface explored for deep deposits with diamond points that cut core samples of rock.

A final economic point concerns the rhythm of development in Victoria. Like California's San Francisco, Melbourne, as the major port and supply centre for the goldfields, was a boom city in the 1850s. And by the 1880s, when it flowered again extravagantly, it had become the centre of Australian mineral investment. It should be remembered also that the 1880s boom received impetus from the movement of population out of the gold towns. There were few opportunities in those towns for the children of the goldrush, who found in Melbourne's new growth similar economic opportunities to those their parents had exploited on the original alluvial fields. That bulge or kink in Victoria's population structure was therefore a powerful economic generator.

DEMOGRAPHIC INFLUENCES
ON THE NEW SOCIETY

Tides of Migration

In terms of population growth and cultural transmission, the 1850s goldrush was a watershed, but mainly in Victoria and through Victoria's influence on the rest of Australia. It is interesting to reflect upon it using an idea from Louis Hartz, an American historian. In *The Founding of New Societies* (1964), Hartz suggests that a migrant society becomes detached from its parent society and is therefore free to develop along new lines. He writes of the migrants as a fragment of their original culture, charged with the ideas dominant in their homeland at the time of foundation and given freedom from the past to explore what he sees as marvellous new possibilities. He argues that the fragment was then cut off from the parent society and from further changes that occurred there. It was in that sense tied to its foundation ideology.

Hartz believes that Australia, as a whole, received a radical fragment, being severed from Britain after the French and industrial revolutions. Our history has therefore been dominated by the working class. The United States, by contrast, was a bourgeois fragment. This interpretation has received critical comment from Australian historians, especially A. W. Martin (1973) who, on the evidence of the predominance of middle-class values, suggests considerable modification, and who points out – against the isolation of the fragment – that strong links were maintained with Britain. Even so, Martin accepts the usefulness of the fragment concept. And the idea of a foundation experience is strong among Australian historians. The continuing influence of the convict era is central to Russel Ward's argument in *The Australian Legend* (1958). Many writers have pointed to the unusual proportions in Australia of the ethnic mix from the British Isles, with particular reference to the strong Irish element. The influence of Scots in the pastoral age of Victoria is powerfully expressed in Margaret Kiddle's *Men of Yesterday* (1961). Relatively poor Lowland farmers at home, they were nevertheless part of a capitalistic operation, during which a few hundred pastoralists secured grazing rights to most of the colony. They were the main actors in what might be called the first foundation of Victoria which was quite different from the pattern suggested by Hartz. Supported by many merchants and bankers, they put up a strong resistance to the new migrant tide that flowed in pursuit of gold.

Because of its strength, which multiplied Victoria's population seven times, and because, especially at first, of its small-man economic system (in contrast to 'the big man's frontier' of pastoralism) the goldrush may helpfully be seen, in Hartz's terms, as a second and contrasting foundation for Victoria. A different land use nourished different values. It was certainly radical. As disturbances on the diggings indicated, there were in this new Victorian 'fragment' numerous Chartists, fresh from confrontation with conservative forces in Britain, as well as a sprinkling of continental revolutionaries and many Americans who believed in colonial independence. They were not only drawn to Australia by gold, but were attracted up-country to a communal life that was at odds with the status divisions of pre-gold society and a system of administration built upon them. Thus began a long struggle in Victoria between the digger migrants and their precursors. It went on throughout the nineteenth century and was institutionalized in a battle for power in parliament. The lower house, representing the newcomers, pressed for change, while the upper house, the stronghold of pastoral and mercantile interests, was frequently successful in blocking progressive legislation.

——————— Goldrush Demography ———————

With these points in mind, the demography of the goldrush is instructive. Victoria was swamped by migrants. Between the censuses of 1851 and 1861 the population grew from 77,345 to 540,322. Arrivals by sea in the decade totalled 572,661 and, subtracting departures, the net migration by sea was 293,319. As often happens in Australia, the internal movement by land was not measured. It would have been considerable for 169,658 of the total was not accounted for by net migration by sea. Children born in the colony (and many would, no doubt, have left with their parents) numbered only about 130,000. It is well known, of course, that many thousands of Chinese were disembarked in South Australia and walked to the goldfields.

The influx did not threaten British dominance of political and cultural life, but it provided an unusual experience for Britons, who had probably never had to mix so freely with foreigners, especially Chinese. As well as Americans, whose influence was large in proportion to their numbers, a Jewish migration, especially from Poland, became significant in business. Main Street at Ballarat was their stronghold. They tended to stay permanently, whereas the majority of foreigners left before 1861. In very rough terms, of 45,410 arrivals from foreign ports, only about one-third (18,439) remained, whereas 251,363 out of 296,768 from Britain were still there.

The characteristics of the migrants were as important as their numbers. Ethnically, Australia remained British. Yet, unlike their general segregation in Great Britain, there was a further mixing of Irish, Scots, Welsh and English, and an interesting cosmopolitan flavour. In Victoria in 1861, there were 10,000 Germans, 8,000 other Europeans and 2,500 Americans.[38] Earlier they had been visible enough to give some credibility to Governor Hotham's claim that foreigners brought about the Eureka Rebellion. Outnumbering all other foreigners, more than 25,000 Chinese became the centre of racial tension, thus beginning a long and sometimes tragic path to the White Australia Policy of 1901. In the late 1850s they were about one-quarter of the digger population on many fields.[39]

From late 1852 the fields became a mosaic of nationalities, many working their own gullies. At Bendigo, according to Frank Cusack[40], there was 'a marked tendency to segregate in national groups'. Long Gully was Bendigo's 'Little Cornwall', Tipperary Gully and the junction of Bendigo and Back Creeks were Irish enclaves, whilst Germans, camped around Ironbark Gully, were the most numerous Europeans. Bendigo was the rallying-point for Germans just as Ballarat was the focus for Americans. Cusack[41] shows that the Germans, who tended to settle permanently, had a long term influence, through their geological skills, in the development of Bendigo's famous quartz mines.

Underdogs in British society, the Irish were favoured by the rough living conditions and manual labour of alluvial mining. On the whole they did not move on into rock mining, in which a later influx of skilled Cornish and Welsh miners was notable. Irish migrants were relatively few in the early 1850s and when more came late in the decade they were faced by restricted opportunities.[42] The Welsh, on the other hand, found in the gold mining towns opportunities for advancement denied them at home. Henry Davies at Ballarat noticed that his previously ill-educated countrymen were being given a great opportunity. They were, by the 1860s, conscious of tremendous benefits from the 'superior social development of Victoria compared with England'.[43]

Apart from number and ethnicity, the characteristics which deserve most consideration about the 1850s migrants were their age, sex, literacy and occupational training, all of which were very significant economically. The youth of the migrants, for instance, as recorded in the census of 1861, contributed to their vitality. Most were in their twenties when they came. If ever the concept of a wave of migrants has had meaning, this was it. As A. R. Hall[44] has argued, they remained as a distinct bulge or kink in Victoria's age structure. As a result, during the 1860s most of the male population was in the workforce and was flexible in adapting to new activity.

That kink in Victoria's age structure had important long-term consequences. Its first effect was in high marriage and birth rates beginning in the late 1850s and continuing through the 1860s. This produced a further bulge when the childen of the gold migrants began their families in the 1880s. Many of them moved (if they had not already done so) from the declining goldfields to opportunities in the growth of Melbourne, where their demand for housing and services was an important cause of that city's boom.

Women were in a minority on the goldfields, especially to begin with. The ratio of European women to men, which was 43:100 in 1857, 56:100 in 1861 and 83:100 in 1871, had an important influence on behaviour. It was much lower than for the colony as a whole, where women were 61 to 100 men in 1857, 70:100 in 1861 and 87:100 in 1871; but, as can be seen, the initial disparity was gradually overcome. New female immigration brought the reunion of family and friends as well as adventurous single women attracted by their prospects in the famous colony.

High Quality Migrants

The adaptability of the migrants seems to reflect not only their youth but also comparatively high levels of education and skill. Although not as cut and dried as age and sex characteristics, which are revealed directly in the census, some clues are available on which to judge their importance. For education, the 1861 census asked whether individuals could read and write, and this can be used roughly, as Geoffrey Serle has done,[45] to indicate comparative literacy. He argues that in 1861:

> . . . only 11 per cent of the European men in Victoria and 22 per cent of the women over twenty-one could neither read nor write – less than half the proportions in the United Kingdom and far better than any other colony or London.

Serle goes on to discuss the quality of the migrants and

concludes by agreeing with a contemporary, Archibald Michie, that Victorians, 'taking an average, were unmistakeably better educated, and more intelligent, than any equal number indifferently taken from the various classes of home society'. On the whole, they had come, unlike the largely poverty-stricken assisted migrants to Australia, from the middle class and better off sections of the working class. As well as their youth, this gave them an entrepreneurial get-up-and-go, which was stimulated by business opportunities in Melbourne, Geelong and on the goldfields.

Their levels of skill are not easily measured, but studies of shipping lists,[46] and the ease with which goldfields communities developed industries, suggest that the reservoir of tradesmen was deep. Skilled workers for the exceptional growth of Ballarat's foundries in the 1850s were found among existing migrants.[47] The scale on which they moved out of mining can be judged from the fact that in 1861 only 29 per cent of males in the workforce at Ballarat West and 49 per cent at Ballarat East were miners. Ten years later the figures were 27 per cent and 33 per cent. Even in the mid-1850s it was misleading to speak just of 'diggers' on the goldfields. With only 43 per cent of the total male workforce, miners' were in a minority at Ballarat West in 1857. The transition had begun early. As noted already Peter Matthews commented in February 1854 that tradesmen at Ballarat were returning to their trades.

As already mentioned there was an important link between this demographic pattern and the economy and society of the goldfields. It is hard to find supporting evidence for Brian Fitzpatrick's claim[48] that a proletariat was probably never created 'so quickly or out of human material so unmalleable' as in the late 1850s and early 1860s in Victoria. Assuming that by proletariat he meant a propertyless, industrially-subjugated working class, the high level of home-ownership alone casts doubt upon his statement. Even so, after the free-for-all, there was a gradual contraction of opportunities. By the 1880s, as Charles Fahey (1982) has shown, at least for Bendigo, many avenues to fortune had closed. As in all capitalist societies, there was a gulf between working miners and mine proprietors. This can, of course, be seen as evidence that entrepreneurial spirits had left the deep workings to a residue for whom there were reasonable wages but no escape into dreamed-of affluence. It was similar at Ballarat. Whereas 89 per cent of miners had owned their own homes in 1870, only 53 per cent did so in 1900.[49] The difference may not be that those who had owned homes in 1870 had lost them, but that many had left mining for more pleasant and profitable undertakings. An immense amount of research is needed before precise statements can be made about the general life history of the goldrush generation.

Religion

A final characteristic of the Victorian population, which had social consequences, was the tendency towards non-conformity in religion. This is measured best from figures recording church attendance rather than answers to the census-takers about formal religious adherence. Even so, the formal pattern showed significant change as indicated in Table 4.

Table 4

Proportion of People of Different Religions in Victoria, Censuses 1851–81

Denomination	1851	1861	1871	1881
Church of England	48.4	39.3	35.3	35.4
Presbyterian	15.0	16.1	15.4	14.4
Methodist	6.5	8.6	12.9	12.8
Other Protestant	5.6	6.5	7.2	7.7
Roman Catholic	23.3	20.3	23.3	23.5
Jewish	0.5	0.5	0.5	0.5
Other	0.8	8.7	5.4	3.9

Source: Census of Victoria.

The growing strength of Wesleyan and Methodist adherence was modest compared to their church attendance. In 1861 they were easily the strongest religious force.

Table 5

Church Accommodation and Attendance, 1861

	Number Churches	Number Buildings Used	Accommodation	Usually Attending
Church of England	73	233	33,638	25,000?
Roman Catholic	59	134	29,844	22,050
Presbyterian (including splinter-groups)	98	163	30,762	18,374
Wesleyan	204	206	36,965	34,140
Other Methodists	89	119	13,858	7,022
Independents	38	45	10,500	7,200
Baptists	28	28	7,579	5,742

Source: Statistics of Victoria, 1861. The Church of England figure for attendance is not given.[50]

This pattern can be linked to crusades over moral issues and the creation of benevolent institutions on the goldfields and in Melbourne.

───────────── Minor Impact of Gold ─────────────

The focus so far on Victoria results not only from its primacy but also from a failure by historians to present an overall picture of the goldrush in New South Wales. Blainey provides part of the picture by indicating that New South Wales had no comparable fields, even in the 1860s. According to Blainey,[51] production in New South Wales during the 1850s was probably only about 7 per cent of Victoria's 26 million ounces, although export figures show 3.7 million ounces. As a result, apart from some migration to Sydney from California, the overwhelming proportion of newcomers to Australia in the 1850s entered through Melbourne. They were drawn particularly by the fame of Mount Alexander (Castlemaine) and Bendigo, then Ballarat. It is likely that in the 1850s the New South Wales fields were exploited mainly by local colonists. Not until the 1860s, with rushes to Kiandra in the Snowy Mountains, then Forbes and Young on the western plains, did many new-comers arrive – and then via Victoria. Some remained for the Gulgong surface rush and Hillend quartz in the early 1870s. People were not deposited nearly as strongly by gold in New South Wales as in Victoria. There was no significant kink in the population structure like that identified by Hall for Victoria. Not only were the yields much poorer and the fields of shorter life, but also the country was drier and less fertile. Little urban development was stimulated. Pastoralism was hardly affected. Although for four years from 1860 to 1863[52] gold exports were worth more than wool, the fleece soon became dominant again in the New South Wales economy. As a consequence, the gold generation in New South Wales was neither socially nor politically of great significance.

INSTITUTIONS AND
BEHAVIOUR

A Special Experience

It would be possible, with no more information than that provided in previous chapters, to speculate fairly accurately about behaviour on the alluvial goldfields. Think of the ingredients: young, adventurous males pursuing easily accessible wealth in up-country areas previously settled sparsely, if at all, and requiring a toughness that excluded gentler spirits from the experience; twenty or thirty thousand of them, at times, on a few hundred hectares of ground; gamblers taking part in a great lottery.

For those who stayed to form permanent communities, the first years were indelible. Decades later the old colonists, as they were usually called, still celebrated that vanished, romantic era and adopted as their emblems the pick, shovel, cradle and dish of the first rushes. As suggested earlier, the only comparable experience in Australian history was that of the 'diggers' (notice the term) of the AIF in World War I.

Those who returned to other lands would have been reminded of the goldrush by books on library shelves. In German, French, Swedish, Norwegian, Italian and, of course, especially in English, diggers themselves and a band of travelling writers described life on the Australian goldfields. Their accounts add up to a considerable literature, which is invaluable source material. William Howitt's *Land Labour and Gold*, Antoine Fauchery's *Letters from a Miner in Australia* (first published in French in 1857), Raffaello

Carboni's *The Eureka Stockade*, William Kelly's, *Life In Victoria*, Ellen Clacy's, *A Lady's Visit to the Gold Diggings of Australia in 1852-3*, and several books by William Westgarth are prominent and diverse examples.

The presence of Ellen Clacy's book in that list is unusual but not surprising. Although the early diggings society was no place for homemaking, many women acted as cooks and tent-keepers for family and friends, or worked in stores, schools, hotels, theatres, restaurants and sly-grog shanties. Sometimes they owned businesses. Most often, commercially, they sold sex. In the free and easy anonymity of the time, they married successful diggers and left them or were deserted by them on casual terms. They proclaimed new found wealth in extraordinary displays of dress. The best silks and satins, unknown to many before, gave great delight. As a Ballarat man wrote about the belle of the ballroom in 1855:

> She dressed sumptuously, and arrayed herself in the hues of the rainbow. Her satin dress, which always looked as if it had been made for somebody else, was overlaid with a massive gold chain, a brooch as big as a warming pan, and a lace collar more costly than clean. Her hands, which were as red as raw beef, and big enough to fell a bullock, were garnished gorgeously with rings; her movements were more energetic than graceful; her language more emphatic than precise; and she was surrounded by an atmosphere redolent of Eau de Cologne, onions and brandy.[53]

Two women in the foreground of S. T. Gill's painting 'Subscription Ball, Ballarat, 1855', might have answered that description.

Like the outback, where women were few, the goldfields enshrined masculine values. Men extended a tradition of mateship and habits of independence, improvization and hard drinking, that Russel Ward has described in *The Australian Legend* (1958). Whether that tradition was passed on by old hands from the pastoral era to the new chums of the golden age has not been demonstrated convincingly. Urban dwellers from Melbourne and Geelong quickly swamped the first Victorian rushes and the overseas contingent had often formed parties of 'ship-mates' during the long voyage. Young and adaptable, they seem to have embraced a camping life that required toughness and improvization. Besides, as far as the central gold-digging experience was concerned, leadership came not from the Australian bush but from California.

The Pioneer Myth

Through the rapid urbanization of the goldfields, the mateship of the early years gave way to a different tradition, that of the pioneer, about which John Hirst[54] has written convincingly. Because mateship was an abstract relationship, with neither temporal nor spatial significance, the concept of the pioneer became dominant in communities which prided themselves on material progress.

The first comers and the original experience were elevated into a mythical past. Once the initial mateship, free-wheeling informality, exciting finds and rough environment had gone forever, most men believed that that was when they had been truly alive. This sentiment, according to one of them, Ballarat's first historian W. B. Withers,[55] led to 'inhabitiveness'. He noticed that many who were successful built permanent homes within sight of a favourite claim or camping place. They took great pride in what they had achieved materially. And because they became segregated from the less fortunate, and could no longer be mates in the original sense, the myth of their great pioneering became dominant. It was strengthened by the foundation of old colonists' clubs with pleasant facilities only available to the better-off. In that way the successful monopolized prestige. Research on Bendigo society suggests that, despite the melting-pot of its alluvial phase, Victorian democracy was not able to achieve the equality of social conditions many original pioneers had dreamed about.[56]

Women were left out of the myth-making and the clubs. The terms 'mate' and 'pioneer' were not themselves sexist, but the power to make use of them was. Men dominated the society and constructed its myths. Yet their strong desire for women, as that other kind of mate, and for homemaking as a base for comfort, caught them up in family life in the 1860s, when a stronger female migration redressed the previous imbalance and when babies, not migrants, were the chief newcomers. The pressures that had forced young girls into prostitution or early marriage gradually eased.[57]

An outcome of the new emphasis on family life was less tolerance of deviant groups, such as prostitutes and the bachelor Chinese. They threatened dreams of a re-birth of Britain, stronger and purer in the new land. By 1870, when the children of the goldrush population explosion at Ballarat were entering their teens, the presence of the Chinese camp and nearby brothels produced a moral frenzy from newspapers and clergymen.[58]

Work

In the goldfields workforce a few women performed tasks unusual for their sex. The census takers of 1861 found that 136 females were mining alongside 78,919 men. Forty-seven, in contrast to 10,692 men, were employed in manufacturing and a handful in the

Table 6

Occupations on the Goldfields, Victoria, 1861

Class	Description	Women	Men
1	Government (administrators, army, navy, police)	5	585
2	Professional (doctors, dentists, nurses)	129	511
3	Professional (teachers, writers, musicians)	488	629
4	Trading (merchants, shopkeepers, bankers, clerks, shop-assistants)	922	5416
5	Personal Offices (hotel, clothing and domestic workers)	6454	4205
6	Manufacturing	47	10,692
7	Goldmining	136	78,919
8	Agriculture	935	7648
9	Carrying	14	3038
10	Food and Drink	522	4906
11	Miscellaneous	45	3001
12	Independent Means	37	132
13	Wives, children	63,295	30,391
14	Prisoners, patients	87	664

Source: Census of Victoria, 1861.

highest professional groups. Their strongest independent role was as shopkeepers, and the only occupations in which they outnumbered men were domestic service and teaching. Table 6 provides a comparison of male and female occupations under general headings derived from the census. It should be noted that in a male workforce totalling 119,682, 78,919 or about two-thirds were in mining; manufacturing was also comparatively strong (because of natural protection). The stimulation of agriculture is indicated in the detailed census tables by the employment of 6663 people on farms in contrast to only 1295 on grazing properties which had been dominant before the gold discoveries.

General Social Results

In assessing the social results of the goldrush, we need to consider the lengthy unsettlement caused by gambling and years of rushing to new finds. Many men became nomads. They followed the gold trail from Victoria to New Zealand and New South Wales or moved into shearing and other part-time pastoral work. Even those who stayed were changed permanently. Booze became an addiction for some who had found it preferable to undrinkable water. Yet it may be that the dramatic confrontations of a government campaign against sly-grog drew more attention to the consumption of hard liquor than was justified. Against the views of some commentators that almost every store sold grog in the days when licensed premises were few, we have to set the fortunes made by soft-drink manufacturers and the huge quantities of tea consumed by Australians.[59]

By any reckoning, however, the extraordinary number of hotels in emerging goldfields towns indicates that the level of drinking was high. How much this was the outcome of habits developed during the rushes is difficult to determine. Echuca, on the pastoral frontier, seems to have had as many hotels.[60] No comparisons are possible because inquiries into levels of drinking were unknown. Nor can there be any precision about the prevalence of sexually transmitted diseases. Advertisements for pills supposed to remedy 'the indiscretions of a hot youth' were numerous in the 1860s and

1870s, but no study has been made of the incidence of syphilis or gonorrhea in goldfields towns. Cases are known of those who suffered the consequences, like Dr Richardson (the father of novelist, Henry Handel Richardson), who died of syphilitic dementia. Of course, this infection may have come accidentally as Dorothy Green points out in *Ulysses Bound*.[61] Henry Handel Richardson's great work *The Fortunes of Richard Mahony* contains a beautifully written account of life on the goldfields. It tells the absorbing story of a restless man, no more at ease in England than in Victoria.

Hotels on the goldfields in the 1850s were places for entertainment as well as for eating and drinking. In the absence of comfortable homes they provided conviviality. After dinner, many merely cleared their largest rooms for performance and then dancing, but some, like Ballarat's Victoria Theatre, attached to the United States Hotel (and now reconstructed at Sovereign Hill), were specially built. The wealth of the diggings attracted some notable artists. G. V. Brooke, a famous Shakespearian actor, and Lola Montez, a notorious courtesan, who performed a frenzied spider dance, shared the stage with comedy, melodrama, excerpts from opera and Christy minstrel shows. Diggers were usually too tired to create songs in the bush tradition. As a result the topical ballad was given a commercial airing. Charles Thatcher, in particular, sang colourfully of local life, with cutting attacks on officials and their procedures. Thatcher, whose career has been explored by Hugh Anderson in *The Colonial Minstrel* (1960), performed mostly at Bendigo. Among other things, he sang of new rushes, to which entertainers flocked as part of the build-up of commercial life on the fields. Only a few weeks after the first rush to Fiery Creek (Beaufort) in 1855, a female tight-rope walker balanced above a crowded street.

The fast buck, the great gamble and the excitement of handling the mineral itself led to fears that gold would spawn the most materialist society on earth. A contemporary moralist asserted that 'Avarice, avarice, alone held undisputed sway'. Towards the end of a powerful discussion about the influence on national character of diggings life, Serle[62] explores the interplay of mercenary and fraternal impulses during which, he believes, the mass experience, with its manliness and mateship, redeemed crude self-interest. In more general terms the driving forces of capitalism were at once stimulated by gold, the economic lubricator, and diverted into a powerful social experience by gold, the democratic mineral. It was an existential experience, frequently valued more for itself than its outcome. As James Bonwick wrote:

> The wild, free and independent life appears the great charm. They have no masters. They go where they please and work when they will. Healthy exercise, delightful scenery, and clear and buoyant atmosphere, maintain an excitement of the spirits, and a glow of animal enjoyment peculiar to bush life.

As already mentioned, the successful pioneers looked back to that time with an affection that softened their materialism. Indeed, there is evidence that gold towns developed an unusual public spirit. In Ballarat, for instance, large gifts to the city of statuary and pictures prompted the proud remark: 'If the successful men of the metropolis showed proportionate generosity and public spiritedness, the Victorian capital would be "marvellous Melbourne" indeed'.[63] It is probably true that the commercial capital city, because of its merchant elite and tradition of borrowing and spending for private show, was more vulnerable to the temptations of Mammon. More importantly, because large areas of crown land were available cheaply for housing under miners' rights, the goldfields were little affected by the kind of land speculation that fuelled Melbourne's 1880s boom.

Clash with the Old Order

Liberated from the formalities and class relationships of their homelands, work-hardened diggers and the storekeepers who supported them were irked by the system of control set up by the central government. Local participation was minimal. Apart from the incorporation of Melbourne and Geelong in the 1840s, there was no local government in Victoria until 1854. Before 1856, when a new constitution granted responsible government, representation was only available in a legislative council through which

English appointed officials made laws. The council was dominated by pre-gold merchants and pastoralists, unsympathetic to the needs of the goldfields. They had a class bias against manual labour and rough behaviour and a fear that their prestige and way of life would be swept away. In defence of mercantile interests, they would not legislate for an export duty on gold, thus forcing the government to continue, against intense opposition, a revenue-raising licence tax on gold diggers.

Enforcement of the tax, especially as it was unrelated to success or failure in winning gold, brought confrontation. This produced many protests, which were the only way the unrepresented goldfields inhabitants could make their feelings and opinions known. Such protests were an opportunity for radicals, like British Chartists, American republicans and continental revolutionaries among the migrants to spread their ideas. It is not surprising, therefore, that after three years of frustration a Reform League appeared at Ballarat towards the end of 1854 to put forward strong proposals for civil liberties and constitutional change. If the League had been heard, the bloodshed of the Eureka Stockade uprising of 3 December 1854 would have been avoided.

Rebellion at Eureka

Explaining Eureka has been a great game for historians and a fascinating puzzle for students about the way the causes of an event can be discussed. Most commentators agree about the underlying conditions. As well as the hated licence tax, these include a social and political gulf between the authorities who administered the fields and those who dug or did business there. On each field, the government camp with its uniformed goldfields commissioners, detachment of regular soldiers, and hard-worked but poorly-trained and often unsavoury police, was set apart from the diggings. Law and order, for which the camp officials were responsible, seemed to be imposed. Although grounded in English common law, legal procedures on the fields were flawed by the appointment of goldfields commissioners as justices of the peace. They could order arrests, prosecute and judge. Offenders were often treated roughly. As a further distortion, the police, many of whom were regarded as corrupt, were offered special incentives to hunt for unlicensed miners and sly-grog sellers.

This situation offended the freewheeling, independent ethos of the diggers. And what was irksome in 1851 and 1852 became intolerable in 1854. There had been an ugly situation at Bendigo in 1853 during a downturn in mining. Protesters wore red ribbons as a revolutionary gesture, refused to pay the licence fee and called for reform.[64] Although some concessions were made, arbitrary rule continued. That it was out of place as the community became more settled may explain why Ballarat, the most permanent and most urbanized field (and until then the most orderly), reached flashpoint late in 1854.

Geoffrey Blainey has drawn attention to the nature of the Ballarat field. He suggests that its deep and wet shafts are the key to understanding the Eureka uprising.[65] They were unpleasant to work, very dangerous and a great financial gamble. Licence hunts disrupted them disproportionately and officials who tried to settle frequent claim disputes were exposed to violent criticism. Officials were unpopular, too, for failing to respond to calls for larger claims in the wet ground where it could take eight months to sink a shaft. Ballarat was also compact, all in the one basin, so that disturbances could quickly become general. A rallying point at Bakery Hill, near the centre of the diggings, had become a traditional protest ground. It was in full view of the camp.

In this special setting general pressures built up during the second half of 1854 causing incidents which widened the distance between the authorities and the diggings community. (Notice the term 'diggings community'. Historians who speak only of diggers neglect the role of storekeepers, tradesmen, lawyers, publicans, doctors and newspapermen.) At first the pressures came from outside Ballarat. A commercial recession brought a crisis in government finance, which a new governor, Sir Charles Hotham, decided to remedy by tough action. Out of touch with the feelings of the diggers, he decided to press hard for the payment of licence fees. In September 1854, when he ordered twice weekly rather than once a month hunts for unlicensed miners, the tension on the fields increased greatly. Because Bendigo, as in 1853, responded much more aggressively than Ballarat, it seems that neither the licence system nor the deep-sinkings were the only keys to the impending disaster.

Unrest at Ballarat focused on the local administration which was less skilful than that at Bendigo.[66] The justice system came under fire when a series of incidents exposed its weaknesses and alienated important groups on the field. The most belligerent and anti-English, the Irish, were outraged by the arrest of their priest's servant on a dubious charge. The Americans protested that a compatriot had been framed by the police for selling sly-grog. The Scots and many others believed that a notorious publican, James Bentley, had been allowed to go free when he should have been charged with the murder of their countryman, James Scobie, outside Bentley's Eureka Hotel. The chairman of the bench, police-magistrate John D'Ewes, who was known to be a friend of Bentley's and was thought to be his business partner, had allowed many irregularities at the committal hearing. As usual, the quickest route to a redress of that grievance was a protest meeting. Held near the hotel, it got out of hand and soon the expensive building was a heap of ashes.

The personal element in the unfolding drama was increased by the response of Robert Rede, Resident Commissioner in charge of the goldfield, who had been on the bench which released Bentley. A pleasant man when not under pressure, he had opposed the continuance of the licence tax and the increased hunts, but developed a belligerent attitude to those who had questioned his authority. Perhaps he thought that the governor expected vigorous action and may have feared for his job if he did not provide it. He expected resistance when arresting those responsible for the hotel burning and wrote to Hotham that, if it came, he wanted to teach the diggers 'a fearful lesson'. Troops were called in from Melbourne and the supposedly civilian administration became an armed camp. The Irish were especially feared. They gathered in armed bands to threaten reprisals for the insult to their priest, as well as expressing anger about the extra licence hunts and adding their weight to the protest over Scobie's case.

An important explanatory point needs to be made. Despite general prosperity at Ballarat, which was in its most productive year, no holes on the Irish-dominated Eureka lead found the gold-bearing gutter for five or six weeks from late August 1854.[67] Well into October the lead was a disaster. Many diggers and store-keepers left for the Gravel Pits. It was just that period that prompt-ed the colourful Italian, Raffaello Carboni, who was working at Eureka, to label the whole of Ballarat as 'a Nugety Eldorado for the few, a ruinous Field of hard labour for many, a profound Ditch of Perdition for Body and Soul to all'. He was wrong; and so is Blainey, who uses the remark as a general assessment of the field.

There are implications here for a general explanation of the con-frontation. It seems that Ballarat's deep-sinkings themselves were not as significant as the situation brought about by deep-sinking on part of the field which by chance was Irish. As in an avalanche, the various elements creating tension put weight on each other. The government stood firm, answering cries for justice with calls for law and order. It responded to unrest with shows of force, follow-ing a pattern of resistance to change that has occurred many times in history. Similarly, drawing upon numerous precedents from English protest movements, a moderate group answered the law and order arguments with claims that the law should be changed to fit altered circumstances. Late in October 1854 they formed the Ballarat Reform League and put forward wide-ranging democratic claims. This can be seen as the gold migrants speaking with a radical voice that was not welcome among officials, who had mer-chant and pastoral sympathies, nor by a strong-minded, naval governor, who had isolated himself from those who might have counselled compromise.

Again, as often happens in such conflicts, there was a symbolic central issue – the fate of three men accused of burning Bentley's Hotel. Although on weak ground legally, the protesters believed that morally the men should be freed. Delegates from a meeting of the Reform League on 23 November carried that message to the governor. Fatefully, by a majority of one, they had been instructed to express their desire as a demand. The voice of the people, they were saying, should be acted upon without question. Hotham bridled at the thought. The use of the word 'demand' turned him cold. While they may have thought that the outcome of a board of inquiry, which had found a senior policeman and John D'Ewes, the police magistrate, guilty of corruption, indicated that their grievances were sound, Hotham probably believed that, in dismissing those men, he had done all that was needed. Not aware that the avalanche was upon him, he stood firm and supported a now belligerent Robert Rede at Ballarat by sending him large troop reinforcements. He encouraged Rede to bring the 'disloyalty' to a head. That was done first by a provocative licence hunt at the peaceful Gravel Pits on Thursday 30 November. Then, when Irish and other dissidents responded by erecting a palisade of slabs at Eureka, it was overrun in the early hours of Sunday 3 December. There was considerable loss of life and outrageous behaviour by the victorious troopers and police.

Rede had certainly isolated the more belligerent and had crushed them. But what the outcome suggests is that the protest movement, which he and Hotham had pushed into a rebellion, was immensely strong. The government was discredited and was never again to assert such authority. A Royal Commission condemned almost everything about the administration of the goldfields. The licence was abolished and a single warden replaced numerous commissioners on each field. The goldfields were given eight members in the legislative council, and the way was open for civil government. By the end of 1855 Ballarat had a municipal council. The drafting of mining regulations, as well as the settlement of claim disputes, was entrusted to an elected local court of mines.

What should we make of it all? Serle sees a fight for freedom.[68] W. B. Withers, the nineteenth-century Ballarat historian, emphasizes the struggle for justice. It was also, you may think, a class issue. The small capitalists, lower middle-class diggers and their storekeeper supporters, representing new money, were in conflict with the pre-gold pastoralists and merchants, men of larger capital who were represented in the legislative council and were sympathetic to the structure of authority imposed on the fields. Sociologically and psychologically drawn together through their communal experience, the newcomers regarded themselves as free spirits whose enterprise was being frustrated by the group they had supplanted. As well as class, then, a conflict of interest groups is discernible.

Blainey stresses the technological by drawing attention to the degree to which the complexity of the field had gone 'beyond the capacity of the law and its representatives to control'.[69] His emphasis is on an underlying revolt of deep-sinkers pursuing economic goals. It is possible to go beyond that to a study of urbanization, and to argue that Ballarat's prosperity and permanence made the administration incongruous and led to the protests that have been described.[70]

In an important sense, Eureka merely regained for the goldfields British civil liberties that three years of makeshift and often arbitrary rule had denied. But it also generated a shock-wave that helped to carry constitutional reforms, like manhood suffrage and vote by ballot, that might otherwise have foundered on the rocks of upper house opposition. As noted, Victoria's legislative council, under the 1855 constitution (implemented in 1856), was able later to delay the achievement of many of the economic and social goals of the gold generation. To the anger of the mining industry, for instance, the legitimation of rights to mine on private property (for minerals to which the crown laid claim) was not achieved until the 1880s. Even so, there were impressive gains. Land selection legislation was comparatively successful, payment of members of parliament was introduced nearly 20 years earlier than in New South Wales and a policy of protection encouraged industry.

British Institutions Transplanted

Once the clash with authority was over and people were more prepared for a long-term commitment to their new communities, many institutions like churches, schools, hospitals, newspapers, mechanics' institutes, libraries, and sporting clubs were founded on the goldfields and strengthened in Melbourne. Local government was introduced. The overall pattern was English but the people who took responsibility would have had no such opportunity in the old world. They pioneered the institutional environment as they had the physical.

A good example of the social dynamics of the period was the performance of the Methodists, whose numbers have already been referred to earlier. Serle[71] explains that they were the only denomination to have striking success on the goldfields, largely because of the initiative they gave to lay preachers and pastoral workers. Their flexibility and their zeal made them very effective. They achieved outstanding attendances. By 1861 Methodists conducted almost as many services as all the other denominations put together. And that was only the beginning. In the 1860s a revival movement lifted their church attendance to almost double that of the nominally much more numerous Anglicans. Methodist historians in Australia have claimed that at no other time or place did their religion make larger or swifter strides.[72] Overall religion was strengthened. Serle[73] states that compared with 1850 double the proportion of the population was attending church regularly in 1861. This earnestness was expressed in serious debates about the meaning of life and embraced a wowserism that for years deadened the sabbath in Victoria and later closed the doors of pubs at 6 pm.

Beginning in the 1860s most Christian denominations had mutual improvement societies, in which young people were encouraged to find a voice about the issues of the day. In the virtual absence of secondary education, those associations assisted personal advancement but, as in Britain, they were mainly promoted as agents of 'citizenship' and 'enlightenment'.[74] The middle-class in the colonial culture turned strongly to youth, being worried about larrikinism arising from unsettled childhood days. There was an answer from those youths, males that is, who joined the Australian Natives Association. From its base as a medical benefits society in the 1870s, the ANA took up many social issues and became a spearhead of the federation cause, which like the ANA flourished in the gold towns.[75]

Frank Cusack[76] has drawn attention to the role of friendly societies on the goldfields. They were particularly important at Bendigo, where almost every adult male belonged. Their strength reflected the lower middle-class origins of the migrants, for whom a thrifty provision for sickness and old age was attractive. Temperance was often also a goal. Groups like the Rechabites, Oddfellows and Foresters were linked to chapters in Britain and organized colony-wide. Most were like modern day service clubs – Apex, Lions, Rotary – in their concern for community projects, and were often the driving force behind annual charity carnivals. The Freemasons, in great vogue at that time in England, seem to have achieved special prestige. One man in three among the successful at Ballarat was a mason. Their moral code, emphasizing benevolence, and their expressed antipathy to class distinction and atheism may have secured them a favoured place in the hearts of the gold generation, but their prominence may also have resulted from careful support for each other in business and civic life. Although Masonry was ecumenical in principle, the fact that Catholics were debarred from membership by their church helped to intensify sectarian feeling.

A Seed Bed for Unionism

Labour unions of national importance emerged during the gold-rush. Among the various strands of unionism transported to Australia, the long-standing craft unions were given an advantage by labour shortages. Stonemasons, who were in very short supply during a building boom in Melbourne, gained an eight-hour working day in 1856. Other craft unions followed, and then shop assistants, whose early-closing campaign sought to reduce week-day hours from as many as fourteen to eight per day. When that was successful, they attacked Saturday late-night shopping. In those days, throughout the community, Sunday was the only day of rest, although a Wednesday or a Saturday half holiday was gradually achieved. From these initiatives a general drive for an eight-hour day emerged. Cusack[77] describes the activity at Bendigo. At Ballarat a United Eight Hours Association was formed in 1874.[78] After 1883 it organized an annual procession and sports meeting through which funds were raised for the erection (in 1886) of a Trades Hall. Then the Eight Hours Association became the Ballarat Trades and Labour Council, which actively supported the extension of the eight-hours principle. Such Trades and Labour Councils were the base from which the Labor Party emerged in the 1890s. It is interesting to note that in proportion to population the push for eight hours in the goldfields towns seems to have been stronger than in Melbourne. The presence of the Amalgamated Miners' Association added special weight.

Miners' unions were slow to form, but when they matured they took over leadership of the labour movement on the goldfields. Quite significantly, there was a basic difference between the Ballarat and Bendigo miners' unions. The Ballarat district model was carefully organized around an accident benefit fund. Originally conceived, though short-lived in Ballarat in 1870, it was re-born through a non-conformist lay-preacher, W.G. Spence, at Creswick, in 1878, and had strong branches at Clunes and Ballarat.[79] It was firm but co-operative with employers.

By contrast, at Bendigo, in a more polarized industrial setting, and under a militant leader, Robert Clark, the miners' union lived by confrontation from its formation in 1872. It fluctuated sharply in numbers according to the level of disputation. Both Clark and Spence dreamed of a colony-wide organization, the first step towards which was taken by Clark in 1874 with the Amalgamated Miners' Association. This was a copy of the National Miners' Association in Britain, where coal mining bred class warfare. In Victoria, in the absence of conflict, its membership fell in the first year from 1832 in twelve branches to 260 in three (Bendigo, Clunes and Stawell). Spence's idea, on the other hand, was fruitful. When the Ballarat union was reformed with 2000 members, in 1880 he had the numbers to take over the Amalgamated Miners' Association and reorganized its branches (including Bendigo in 1882) along accident benefit lines. All the funds were consolidated and clearance cards issued so that miners could move without disadvantage from district to district. Even so, according to Cusack[80], the union was weak at Bendigo because of the strength of friendly society medical benefits.

Spence went further by forming an Australasian organization of miners' unions, and then by founding a shearers' union. In the Creswick-Ballarat area many men moved between mining, forest work, farming and shearing. Miners and shearers were the vanguard of a new style of unionism, which Spence and David Temple (his right hand man with the shearers) exported from the Victorian goldfields to pastoral New South Wales. In an immense expansion in that colony, sheep numbers grew from six to about sixty million between 1860 and 1890. In the same time in Victoria the flock merely doubled from six to twelve million.[81] In what he termed New Unionism, Spence extended the movement to all pastoral workers by enrolling shed and station hands in the Australian Workers' Union, the first large-scale union of unskilled workers in the world. Although still based on a benefits fund and espousing Christian values of brotherly love, which Spence compared to mateship, this new style of unionism was to take on greater militancy from the more polarized pastoral situation in New South Wales and Queensland. During the 1890s strikes, Ballarat's Eureka flag could be seen flying over camps of armed shearers, many of whom were land selectors who had once, perhaps, been diggers.

Such long term institutionalized social results of the goldrushes are sometimes overlooked. They indicate how attitudes and ideas interact with social and economic structures in a cultural transmission that is more complicated than Louis Hartz suggests in *The Founding of New Societies*. Victoria's 'radical fragment' derived a liberal, self-improving tone from goldrush opportunities. The influence of the pioneer experience lay deep in the social fabric, as an acceptance, whether justified or not, that everyone had had an equal chance.

In terms of politics, there was no seed bed for the Labor Party in the goldfields towns. In contrast, the social climate and soil of New South Wales nurtured the Victorian seed of New Unionism to produce a strong crop of country Labor members of Parliament in 1891.

URBANIZATION

A Neglected Phenomenon

Urbanization, one of the most important results of the Victorian goldrush, is the most neglected. In over thirty pages about economic redirection between 1851 and 1861, Serle[82] spares perhaps thirty lines for strictly urban matters. He notes that because of natural protection the towns built on gold were flourishing in 1861, when Melbourne and Geelong were depressed, but attempts no overview of their development. Urban history throughout the world was little valued when he was writing and the use of easily established, export-import measures of economic output hid the strength of urban growth in Australia until N.G. Butlin (1962), with a team of researchers, put together figures suitable for an historical analysis of gross national product. Since then, the capital cities have received greater attention in writings such as those of Burnley (1974), Davison (1978), Glynn (1970), but little has been done to look at towns up-country. As I indicated in 'The Urban Sprinkle',[83] regional historians have not given country towns their due.

The general picture should have been clear from census returns. In Victoria, people were drawn up-country by gold and many remained there in towns which became significant market and industrial centres. The fall in Melbourne's share of colonial population from 38 per cent in 1851 to 23 per cent in 1861 is a rough indication of their gain. And although the capital pulled back slowly to 26 per cent in 1871, 31 per cent in 1881 and (finally eclipsing its pre-gold dominance) to 41 per cent in 1891, for the first and only time in Australian history a sizeable population was permanently located inland. In 1861, when there were still about 100,000 miners, the goldfields held 228,000 people in comparison with 125,000 in Melbourne; and in 1871 when Melbourne had grown to 191,000, there were over 270,000 people on the gold-fields of whom 146,000 (a powerful balancing urban force) were in towns of over 500. Although there was a large drift to Melbourne, which made prodigious growth in the 1880s, the gold towns still held 144,000 people in 1891. Their prominence can still be under-stood, especially in the central highlands, where fine buildings are evidence of an unusual past.

The intensity of mining created instant townships. Some dis-appeared just as quickly, but many moved from canvas to wooden structures and then to brick and stone. As explained earlier, the surface phase of digging produced the least permanence. The win-nings of Bendigo's great days under canvas in 1852 and 1853 were taken elsewhere, leaving a small but neat and orderly nucleus for further growth when a permanent town site was surveyed in 1854.[84] In 1855, by contrast, Ballarat was a mess. A vast amount of business was being done in a quagmire along the road to Geelong, among the deep-sinkings of the Gravel Pits. Louisa Meredith[85] found it 'more irredeemably hideous than the blackest mining vil-lage in any English coal or iron district'. But it was on the way to dazzling growth in the emergence of Main Street, Ballarat East, which has been described and explained in *Lucky City*.[86]

Although the most remarkable urban phenomenon of the 1850s, Main Street became, for much of its length, a ghost street by the 1870s. The westward movement of mining and the arrival of the railway from Geelong had ended its role as Ballarat's main enter-tainment and shopping centre and point of entry for goods from the coast. Many of its buildings have been reconstructed at Sovereign Hill from plans connected with the survey of the road and elevations taken from lithographs of the period. The recovery of its social fabric from newspapers, reminiscences, ratebooks and surveyors' plans suggests abundant life and a cosmopolitan flavour unusual for nineteenth-century Australia.

Ballarat's relocation westwards, on the grid plan of a township site originally surveyed in 1852 and almost free of surface mining, not only caused a decline in Main Street but also fostered a new and more substantial boom as the gold streams were followed under basalt rock. Already by 1862, the location for ten foundries, several cattleyards, a haymarket, railway terminus, major banks and hotels, this Ballarat West community matured by 1871 into a city that surprised the English novelist Anthony Trollope because it was so solidly built and so well-endowed with hospital, libraries, hotels, public gardens and other amenities. He found a contrast with crowded, unfinished, uncomfortable Bendigo, which was what he expected a mining town to be. Bendigo's quartz boom, which greatly stimulated industry and commerce, was just beginning. Blinded by English experience of the growth of industrial cities on rivers, which provided cheap water transport, Trollope failed to understand that natural protection had added immeasurably to the golden base of Ballarat's economy.

The Basis of Urban Growth

The speed and scale of urbanization varied according to the nature and stage of exploitation of gold deposits. Ballarat and Bendigo again provide a classic contrast, which has been emphasized in *Lucky City*.[87] The relevant passage is worth reproducing:

> The total amount recovered by 1871 (Ballarat 9.2 million oz and Bendigo 6.6 million oz) could possibly have been responsible for the difference between the two places. But it seems unlikely. A more powerful influence was the timing of the gold finds. Bendigo's extraordinary surface alluvial phase in 1852-4 hardly contributed to urban development. Because of rough conditions, little of the gold was ploughed back into local facilities. On the other hand, Ballarat's early production was highest from 1854 to 1858, when town life was developing rapidly and those who had come to dig were ready to settle. And when this was capped in the sixties (see table) by the production of 5 million oz (against Bendigo's 2 million) Ballarat's urban advantage was immense.

Period	Ballarat (oz)	Bendigo (oz)
1851–60	4,262,000	4,521,000
1861–70	5,000,000	2,128,000
Total	9,262,000	6,649,000

This was a powerful influence. But just as strong was the nature of Ballarat's gold deposits, which ensured the dominance of local capital and helped an extraordinarily self-reliant community to develop. For twenty years the same people were committed to the famous leads, at first as miners and storekeepers, later in all walks of life. The energies and resources of the community were so concentrated upon the mines that the profits of the 1856 mining boom were gradually ploughed back during the slump from 1859 to 1863, when incredible difficulties, both physical and financial, were overcome. This investment, often a sacrifice, was inspired by a blind faith which only gold could have planted in the whole community.

In these terms the romance of Ballarat's rapid but solid growth can only be explained as luck or geological determinism. The initial concentration of leads in the Ballarat East basin held the miners in proximity to the planned town, which by another chance was perfectly situated for further growth when the rock-leads were exploited. Then a long period of waiting tested and refined techniques and attitudes until finally the bonanza of the mid-sixties gave people the opportunity to erect substantial houses and business premises which had previously been out of the question.

Industrialization was an important element of urbanization. Natural protection gave industries on the goldfields a boost that was to sustain them for decades. In the major towns large foundries supplied equipment not only to local mines but also to those on smaller fields. The machinery orders for mines participating in the quartz phase at Stawell, for instance, which Murray and White[88] explain had 'to all intents and purposes become an outpost of the Ballarat Mining Exchange', were placed by their Ballarat managers with Ballarat metal works. Bendigo's industries profited similarly when quartz boomed in the 1870s and the city matured. Castlemaine boasted Thomson's foundry. One of the most prosperous and efficient in the colony, it diversified out of mining into

POPULATION OF VICTORIAN GOLD TOWNS, 1871

Ballarat ⊙ 47,201

Bendigo ⊙ 28,577

Castlemaine ⊙ 5,000 – 7,500
Daylesford ⊙ 2,500 – 5,000
Chewton ⊙ 1,000 – 2,500
Carisbrook • 500 – 1,000

Table 7

Population of Victorian and New South Wales Gold Towns, 1871

Victoria		New South Wales	
Ballarat	47,201	Mudgee	1786
Bendigo	28,577	Grenfell	1657
Castlemaine	6935	Forbes	1276
Clunes	6068	Adelong	864
Stawell	5166	Hillend	716
Daylesford	4696	Trunkey Creek	681
Creswick	3969	Sofala	644
Maldon	3817		7624
Maryborough	2935		
Amherst	2878		
Beechworth	2866		
Chewton	2387		
Ararat	2370		
Browns (Scarsdale)	2121		
Buninyong	1981		
Heathcote	1554		
Dunolly	1553		
Walhalla	1484		
Graytown	1422		
Tarnagulla	1359		
Malmsbury	1357		
Chiltern	1212		
Inglewood	1189		
St Arnaud	1101		
Woods Point	1059		
Steiglitz	1058		
Smythesdale	1003		
Carisbrook	941		
Wedderburn	862		
Beaufort	780		
Avoca	768		
Rutherglen	616		
Linton	595		
Raywood	528		
Yackandandah	553		
Trentham	517		
	145,978		

Note: Towns with populations above 500 and with over 40 miners in the workforce. Ballarat includes Sebastopol and Bendigo includes Eaglehawk.
Source: Censuses of New South Wales and Victoria, 1871.

the production of boilers and equipment for other industries. The Phoenix foundry at Ballarat became highly specialized. Against local and Melbourne competition in 1871, it gained the initial Victorian government contract for steam locomotives. It dominated that field for seventeen years, producing 200 locomotives, half of them in just five years from 1883 to 1888.[89] These examples indicate the quality of Victorian up-country urbanization. Its scale in contrast with New South Wales is striking. Table 7 shows that for 1871 fifteen Victorian gold towns were larger than their largest counterpart in New South Wales. In Victoria there were 36 towns with populations over 500 and with more than 40 gold-miners in the workforce; in New South Wales there were only seven.

———— The Importance of Victoria's Gold Towns ————

When considering Victoria there has been a tendency, through hindsight linked to Melbourne's dominance, to think of 'Melbourne and the rest'. But it is salutary to consider the gold region as an entity. As an urban experience the 36 towns in Table 7 were a remarkable balancing force. They held 145,978 people in 1871 compared with 191,000 in Melbourne. It could be argued that through to the end of the century the former goldfields and their hinterlands (they held a total population in 1871 of 270,428) were almost as powerful socially and culturally as Melbourne. We have relied too much on central records and a centralized tradition to understand their strength. Writers like Serle (1971), assuming the primacy of Melbourne and focusing attention there, have distorted the picture of late nineteenth-century Victoria.

Butlin[90] is misleading in a different way in his account of the urban element in the Australian economy. In pointing to the growth of New South Wales towns and the decline of Victorian towns in the period after 1861 by reference to population alone, he fails to understand that such a comparison can be made only for similar types of towns at similar stages of growth. Ballarat, for example, was stable in population from 1871 to the end of the century but grew vigorously in every other way – with better factories, greater horsepower, bigger houses, more handsome public buildings, superior facilities and an increasingly skilled workforce. Contrast that with a rather miserable group of mainly pastoral towns in New South Wales holding populations of 500 or so. They had indeed grown but showed little capacity to generate capital or sustain industry. Their men were often away in the nomadic workforce and many contained a high proportion of dependent women. This does not suggest, as Butlin claims, that the urban initiative had passed from the south. The Phoenix foundry's locomotives and McKay's Harvesters (many hundreds of them) are almost evidence enough of his failure to consider the typology of the towns.

It should not be surprising, in terms of this discussion of urbanization, that the most powerful myth in Victoria, the myth of 'Marvellous Melbourne', should have been an urban one, in contrast to the bush myth centred principally on Sydney. Speed and scale of growth and quality of life, its chief ingredients, were found equally on the goldfields, from which there was a large migration to Melbourne during the 1880s boom. This suggests that Melbourne emerged as a metropolis as part of a general consciousness of town life in Victoria and a great pride in the material achievements of the gold migrants.

There were symbols of that achievement throughout the gold region. Bendigo's town centre, with its magnificent Law Courts and Shamrock Hotel,[91] was the most elegant. But Ballarat produced a set of self-images that is very instructive. It was labelled 'Golden City' in response to 'Marvellous Melbourne' and claimed an almost heroic public spirit that its champions believed could not be matched at the centre. The *Ballarat Courier* argued in 1890:

> . . . If the successful men of the metropolis showed proportionate generosity and public spiritedness, the Victorian capital would be 'Marvellous Melbourne' indeed . . . surely it marks a very desirable development that the most famous goldfield that the world has known should become the 'city of trees', and then achieve a nobler title still, the 'city of statues', and pictures.[92]

Alongside their powerful radical influence on mainstream liberalism and their prominence in the federation cause the gold towns were the core of an up-country urban experience that has differentiated Victoria from all other Australian communities.

POLITICAL AND CULTURAL
OUTCOMES

────────── How Powerful Was Gold ──────────

There has been an interesting argument among historians about the overall consequences of the goldrushes. Until 1955 the accepted view was that they produced a new Australia. Then in *Australia: A Social and Political History*, R. M. Hartwell and I. D. McNaughtan, in separate chapters, claimed that the effects of gold had been greatly exaggerated.* Hartwell[93] maintained 'there was no spectacular change of direction, either in politics or economy, with the discovery of gold'. He added 'The pastoralist, more than anyone else, has moulded the development of Australia'. In the same vein, McNaughtan[94] claimed that 'the diggers era left a fainter impress on Australian life than the first ten years of the squatting age'. He conceded a large influence but not a transformation:

> Gold trebled the population in ten years, brought enormous and sudden wealth, and gave a greater complexity to colonial society and a powerful impulse to existing trends. Yet it does not seem that this fabulous windfall diverted the course of Australian development from the broad lines laid down before 1851.

In a cautious reply, Geoffrey Serle rounded off his study of Victoria's 'golden age' by conceding McNaughtan's overall claim about

---

* Economic historians N. G. Butlin (1984) and W. A. Sinclair (1976) have supported this view from an economic standpoint.

the fainter impress of the diggers' era, but contended: 'it is certainly not true of Victoria – which until the dying days of the century held over one-third of the Australian population'. He went on to point out that 'the lifting of Victoria from obscurity to numerical and economic predominance' was a fundamental change from what McNaughtan called 'the broad lines laid down before 1851'.[95]

Similarly in politics, Serle[96] pointed out that, in a manner unique to Victoria, the gold towns were the driving force of the democratic movement during the 1850s. As you might conclude from the discussion of up-country urbanization, it was the same in the 1860s and 1870s when all the major political programs – selection, protection, payment of members of parliament, education and constitutional reform – were of vital importance to the development and beliefs of those communities. The parliament was a special battleground because the Victorian constitution of 1855 gave the pastoralist and propertied upper house the power to frustrate the wishes of the new migrants, represented in the lower house. Victoria was unusual in developing a radical-liberalism, nowhere stronger than on the goldfields, in which working class and middle class interests combined to press for social justice and equality of opportunity. Individualism was blended with public spiritedness. As Serle has said[97], the diggers were both evangelists for Chartism* and men in pursuit of material gain. Their experience of opposing authoritarian rule on the early goldfields was built in to their stance.

─────────── **The Spread of Victorian Influence** ───────────

Sometimes historians argue over red herrings. When Serle[98] agreed with R. M. Hartwell's[99] criticism of an earlier view that there was a 'conservative plantation tradition' in New South Wales and a 'democratic camp-frontier tradition' in Victoria, he was talking

---

* Chartism was an English program of political reform. The People's Charter, adopted in 1838, called for manhood suffrage, equal electoral areas, no property qualifications for and payment of members of parliament, vote by ballot and annual parliaments.

about politics and therefore essentially focusing on the terms *conservative* and *democratic*. It is unlikely that he was conceding that there were not different traditions in the two colonies. For, because of gold, the eight-hours movement and a specially organized shearers' union became the means by which a Victorian brand of unionism was exported to New South Wales. It moved from the mining frontier to the pastoral frontier – the original terms 'camp' and 'plantation' are, of course, misleading – with consequences of vast significance in Australian history. Whether the mining strand which produced it or the pastoral strand which received it was more important is hard to determine, but it can be argued that Victorian union influence, and especially the activity of W.G. Spence, was critical in the lead-up to the 1890s strikes in New South Wales and Queensland where the majority of Australia's sheep were grazed. Further, bush unionism in New South Wales provided an organizational base for the election in 1891 of nineteen Labor members of parliament in country seats, thereby helping to establish what has become a major difference between New South Wales and Victoria. The former has been the stronghold of Labor, which has not only dominated state politics but has also been the power base for Labor prime ministers of Australia. By contrast, Victoria has been strongly liberal, out of the liberal-radical gold-rush tradition, and has provided the majority of non-Labor prime ministers.

What has to be said most strongly is that throughout eastern Australia there were new and massive interactions because of gold. Although the political tide flowing before 1851 in the cities might have brought democracy, as McNaughtan argues,[100] the social groups through whom it flowed would have been much weaker and the confidence of the democracy greatly reduced without the democratic mineral. Unionism was not the only export from the goldfields to the pastoral outback. Many people went, taking with them the tradition of Eureka that set the Southern Cross flag flying above shearers' camps in the 1890s. They also took racist attitudes from their contact with the Chinese. We do not know how many people with Victorian experience moved into the outback of New South Wales and Queensland. The census did not record internal migration. But it is probable that pastoralism would not have expanded so successfully between 1851 and 1890 without bush-hardened men from the Victorian diggings. Reinforcements had to come from outside the area because total fertility in the predominantly masculine pastoral frontier was minimal. We do know, from G. L. Buxton's study of the Riverina (1967), that Victorians were prominent among selectors and townsfolk in that region. It is clear that because the Riverina was economically tied to Victoria there was so much trade across the border that the customs levies and stock taxes payable there became an irksome burden. To bring the two colonies together in a customs union became a major aim of nationalists seeking the federation of the Australian colonies.

Federation

The existence, as a result of the goldrushes, of two outstanding colonies, balanced in economic power, probably gave a major impetus to the federal movement. Neither could dominate it and, if both came in, it would be folly for the smaller colonies to stay out. Of the two, Victoria was more enthusiastic for federation. Pastoral and mining investment across the continent gave Victorians a broad view; their families as well as their money were on the move. They had also shown a national spirit in union organization and had spawned the Australian Natives Association, with great strength on the goldfields and a passion for federation. When it came to a vote, the gold towns of Victoria were the strongest pro-federation electorates in the land. Both Ballarat and Bendigo recorded a 95 per cent 'Yes' vote at the federal referendum of 1898. Victoria as a whole was 86 per cent in favour, compared with 52 per cent in New South Wales and 67 per cent in South Australia.

Cultural Patterns

In broad cultural terms the goldfields seem to have generated in Victoria an institutional approach to society and the arts that had no parallel in New South Wales. Coming early in the history of the colony and injecting great new wealth and energy, gold gave an opportunity to found a university, art gallery, museum, library and many professional societies.[101] Victorians were very conscious of the need to build strong structures on which the arts and sciences might grow. In the same vein the legislative council in 1854 set aside large grants of money for religious bodies to found secondary schools, which were to act as a bulwark against the flood of democracy.[102] Because the democracy was so middle-class in aspiration, this institutional initiative became the cornerstone of a system of private (independent) education in Victoria that remains the strongest in the nation. In Sydney today, so it is said, people ask how much you earn, in Melbourne what school you went to.

Bernard Smith has argued[103] that by a conscious effort Melbourne 'was able quite early in its history to develop a fine arts system on the Renaissance model'. It was strong on education and conservation. Sydney, on the other hand, developed in a more narrowly professional way. 'Its strength came to lie not in its educational but in its marketing components.' Jim Davidson[104] puts it another way – that Melbourne has tended to the classical and institutional, Sydney to the romantic and individualist.

The same thing can be seen on the goldfields. At Ballarat in 1884, Australia's first provincial fine art gallery was founded.[105] That art gallery, given a splendid building in 1890, seems to have been chiefly supported by men who had been aware of art before their migration and were concerned to provide their community with an institution comparable to those from which they had benefited themselves. But with this qualification, that the chief promoter and benefactor was the Wesleyan, James Oddie, a life-long democrat, who prevented the gallery becoming just an echo of Europe by stimulating local art and by building in the myth of the pioneers. He commissioned dozens of portraits of old diggers and landscapes, including a magnificent von Guerard, of the early goldfield. He secured the original Eureka flag for the gallery and started an annual exhibition by amateurs, in the first of which appeared a landscape by Percy Lindsay of Creswick, the eldest of a remarkable artistic family. Their grandfather had used the gallery to educate them in art.

As part of a general concern to improve the community, a

unique society, secular and male like the ANA, emerged at Ballarat in 1879. Called the Ballarat Young Men's General Debating Society, it built its own hall at South Street in 1886 and in 1890 began an annual literary, debating and musical competition that soon drew thousands of participants from all over Australia. Greatly extended, it still exists under the name of the South Street Society. From a democratic tradition, with its roots in Welsh eisteddfods, it turned its back on the possibility of becoming exclusive, like world-famous Bayreuth.

There is an important point of reference in the 1850s for a different art tradition in Victoria. The publisher Thomas Ham worked closely with the artist S. T. Gill to provide lithographs that migrants could send home as evidence of their diggings experience. This was people's art, showing the ordinary life of the lower middle-class and could be achieved because of their relative wealth. It was so far from the conventional that in associated watercolours Gill broke away from European influence to record the blue and gold tones of the Australian bush, not fully realized until Roberts, Streeton, McCubbin and others of the Heidelberg school painted in the open air during the 1880s. To do so they camped out as Gill had done; and their search for archetypal bush characters and experience is consistent with a stream of artistic endeavour stretching back to the goldfields. In conjunction with the institutional strength of art in Victoria, it is not surprising that exploration of Australian life through painting should have been so strong in Victoria.[106]

There was a different emphasis in literature. Whereas in Victoria the goldfields experience, with its urban outcome, had supported professional entertainers and artists, the pastoral frontier of New South Wales, with its campfires and men's huts, stimulated balladists. They continued a strong tradition, unbroken since convict days. It was lifted to national importance by a magazine, the *Bulletin*, and a writer, Henry Lawson, both of them distinctively products of New South Wales and its weaker goldrush. Lawson was born on the Grenfell goldfield in 1867 and was fated to share the marginal existence of his carpenter father on a miserable selection near Gulgong, where moderately rich surface diggings were worked in the early 1870s.

Lawson moved to Sydney in his teens and, after exposure to the republican movement, wrote aggressive verse, in a spirit foreign to Victoria. Lawson became famous for short stories about the battlers he had known in his childhood, or met later when he was sent to the pastoral outback by the *Bulletin*. Nothing like his work came out of Victoria.

Both the republican and bush strands in Lawson's writing and the Sydney *Bulletin* itself had little influence, according to Serle,[107] in the southern colonies. There the emphasis was on pioneers rather than mates and on material achievement rather than personality. As a result, Sydney became the home of the bush myth in Australia and 'Marvellous Melbourne' the chief expression of an urban myth. Republican influence seems also to have made the people of New South Wales more Australian in sentiment. The *Bulletin* proclaimed 'Australia for the Australians' from its masthead, whereas in places like Ballarat the pioneers thought of themselves strongly as Britons. This did not mean that Victorians were unaware of themselves as Australians, but that being Australian, and having done what they had, they thought of themselves as the best of Britons. They did not want to alter allegiances as Republicans did, but to build on them. This meant that to the family-making, goldrush migrant generation, who had left their mothers behind forever in pursuit of personal gain, Queen Victoria became more strongly than elsewhere a sentimental mother figure. They were proud that the colony named after her had developed so remarkably almost entirely in her reign.

That pride expresses in microcosm the mental experience of those who settled in Victoria during the 1850s. It indicates that the kink in Victoria's age structure was a powerful social force. Through the economic stimulus of the goldrush and especially its small-scale capitalism Victorians were elevated briefly into a favoured place in Australian history. Their way of looking at things gave Australia a special injection of radical-liberalism and planted in the south of the continent artistic, educational and social institutions that have had a significant long-term influence. Thus, although gold as a product may have had a short life as the most powerful element in the Australian economy, its pump-priming role in industrialization, urbanization and in the diversification of

the rural sector released the energies of an unusually gifted generation of migrants, whose economic contribution cannot be quan-
tified just in terms of the production of gold. As Australia is
finding out to its cost in the 1980s, a well-educated and skilled
population is a vital economic resource.

NOTES

1. Blainey 1963: 62.
2. Blainey 1963: 42.
3. N. G. Butlin 1962; Butlin and Sinclair 1986.
4. S. J. Butlin 1986: 8.
5. Buxton 1967: 15-55.
6. Cusack 1973: 111, 133-4.
7. Blainey 1963: 45.
8. McCarty 1974: 11-13.
9. Bate 1978: 118.
10. Bate 1978: 122.
11. Blainey 1963: 42.
12. Serle 1963: 41, 220-1; Blainey 1963: 66-71.
13. Serle 1963: 224.
14. Cusack 1973: 130.
15. Bate 1978: 202.
16. Cusack 1973: 137, 148-52.
17. Butlin and Sinclair 1986: 132.
18. Serle 1963: 239-40.
19. Serle 1963: 241.
20. Bate 1978: 41.
21. Bate 1978: 96-113.
22. Cusack 1973: 175-6.
23. Serle 1963: 231.
24. Barnard 1962: 32-6.
25. Priestley 1965: 32-6.
26. Serle 1963: 229.
27. *Ballarat Star*, 19 June 1871, p. 2.
28. Serle 1963: 232.
29. Bate 1978: 118.
30. Bate 1978: 131-2.
31. Serle 1963: 235-9; Blainey 1966: 231.
32. Blainey 1966: 235.
33. Serle 1963: 239.
34. Butlin 1959.
35. Serle 1963: 239.
36. Serle 1963: 237-8.
37. Serle 1963: 237.
38. Serle 1963: 371.
39. Serle 1963: 389.
40. Cusack 1973: 55.
41. Cusack 1973: 58.
42. Serle 1963: 247-8, 372.
43. Bate 1978: 84, 91, 148.
44. Hall 1963.
45. Serle 1963: 371-2.
46. Morrissey 1966.
47. Bate 1978: 128, 147; Cope: 52-6.
48. Fitzpatrick 1946: 56.
49. Bate 1978: 190.
50. From Serle 1963: 343.
51. Blainey 1963: 84.

52. Blainey 1963: 84.
53. Bate 1978: 104.
54. Hirst 1978: 316-37.
55. Withers 1887: 194.
56. Fahey 1982.
57. Bate 1978: 146.
58. Bate 1978: 156.
59. Dingle 1980: 243.
60. Priestley 1965: 66.
61. Green 1973: 23.
62. Serle 1963: 94.
63. *Ballarat Courier*, 13 June 1890.
64. Cusack 1973: 87-97.
65. Blainey 1963: 46.
66. Cusack 1973: 104-5.
67. Bate 1978: 51-55.
68. Serle 1963: 181.
69. Blainey 1963: 51.
70. Bate 1978: 41-2.
71. Serle 1963: 342-3.
72. Benson 1935: 343.
73. Serle 1963: 343.
74. Bate 1978: 228.
75. Serle 1971: 231-6.
76. Cusack 1973: 169-70.
77. Cusack 1973: 140-2.
78. Bate 1978: 263.
79. Bate 1978: 261.
80. Cusack 1973: 169-70.
81. Butlin 1962: 284-5.
82. Serle 1963: 216-48.
83. Bate 1974: 106-7.
84. Cusack 1973: 72-3.
85. Meredith 1861: 243.
86. Bate 1978: 96-113.
87. Bate 1978: 114.
88. Murray and White 1983: 37.
89. Bate 1978: 213-15.
90. Butlin 1964: 186-92.
91. Cusack 1973: 195.
92. *Ballarat Courier*, 13 June 1890.
93. Hartwell 1955: 47.
94. McNaughtan 1955: 98.
95. Serle 1963: 380.
96. Serle 1963: 380.
97. Serle 1963: 380.
98. Serle 1963: 380.
99. Hartwell 1955: 47.
100. McNaughtan 1955: 102.
101. Serle 1963: 351-68.
102. Serle 1963: 350-51.
103. Smith 1986: 170.
104. Davidson 1986: 230.
105. Bate 1978: 228.
106. Astbury 1985.
107. Serle 1973: 60.

BIBLIOGRAPHY

Anderson, H. 1960. *The Colonial Minstrel*, Melbourne.

—— 1969. *The Flowers of the Field: A History of Ripon Shire*, Melbourne.

Astbury, L. 1985. *City Bushmen. The Heidelberg School and The Rural Mythology*, Melbourne.

Austin, K. A. 1967. *The Lights of Cobb and Co*, Adelaide.

Bate, W. 1974. 'The Urban Sprinkle', in C. B. Schedvin and J.W. McCarty (eds.), *Urbanization in Australia: The Nineteenth Century*, Sydney.

—— 1978. *Lucky City: The First Generation at Ballarat, 1851-1901,* Melbourne.

Benson, C. I. (ed.) 1935. *A Century of Victorian Methodism*, Melbourne.

Blainey, G. 1961. 'Gold and Governors', *Historical Studies*, 36, May.

—— 1958. *Gold and Paper. A History of the National Bank of Australasia,* Melbourne.

—— 1962. 'The Gold Rushes: The Year of Decision', *Historical Studies*, 38, May.

—— 1963. *The Rush That Never Ended*, Melbourne.

Bonwick, J. 1942. *Notes of a Gold Digger and Gold Digger's Guide,* Melbourne.

Broome, R. 1984. *The Victorians. Arriving*, Sydney.

Butlin, N. G. 1962. *Australian Domestic Product, Investment and Foreign Borrowing*, Cambridge.

—— 1986. *Bicentennial Perspective of Australia's Economic Growth*, The Economic History Society of Australia and New Zealand.

—— 1959. 'Colonial Socialism in Australia, 1860-1900', in H.G.J. Aitken (ed.), *The State and Economic Growth*, New York.

—— 'Contours of the Australian Economy, *Australian Economic History Review*, XXXI (2).

—— 1964. *Investment in Australian Economic Development, 1861-1900*, Cambridge.

Butlin, N. G. and Sinclair, W. A. 1986. 'Australian Gross Domestic Product 1788-1860: Estimates, Sources and Methods', *Australian Economic History Review*, XXVI (2).

Butlin, S. J. 1986. *The Australian Monetary System 1851-1914*, Judith F. Butlin.

Buxton, G. L. 1967. *The Riverina*, Melbourne.

Carboni, R. 1963. *The Eureka Stockade*, Melbourne (1855).

Clacy, E. 1963. *A Lady's Visit to the Gold Diggings of Australia in 1852-3*, London (1853).

Cope, G. 1971. 'Some aspects of the Development of the Metal Trades in Ballarat 1851-1901', M.A. Thesis, University of Melbourne.

Cronin, K. 1982. *Colonial Casualties. Chinese in Early Victoria*, Melbourne.

Currey, C. H. 1954. *The Irish at Eureka*, Sydney.

Cusack, F. 1973. *Bendigo: a History*, Melbourne.

Davidson, J. 1986. Introduction to *The Sydney Melbourne Book*, Melbourne.

Davison, G. J. 1978. *The Rise and Fall of Marvellous Melbourne*, Melbourne.

Dingle, A. E. 1980. 'The truly magnificent thirst: an historical survey of Australian drinking habits', *Historical Studies*, 75, October.

Dingle, T. 1984. *The Victorians: Settling*, Sydney.

Fahey, C. 1982. 'Wealth and Social Mobility in Bendigo and Northern Victoria 1879-1901', Unpublished Ph.D Thesis, University of Melbourne.

Fauchery, A. 1965. *Letters from a Miner in Australia*, Trans, Melbourne (1857).

Fitzpatrick, B. 1946. *The Australian People, 1788-1945*, Melbourne.

—— 1949. *The British Empire in Australia: An Economic History 1834-1939*, Melbourne.

Flett, J. 1956. *Dunolly*, Melbourne.

Gill, S. T. 1852. *Victorian Gold Diggings As They are*, Melbourne.

Glynn, S. 1970. *Urbanisation in Australian History, 1788-1900*, Adelaide.

Gollan, R. 1960. *Radical and Working Class Politics: A Study of Eastern Australia, 1850-1910*, Melbourne.

Government of Victoria, 1854-5. 'Report of the Commission Appointed to Inquire into the Condition of the Goldfields of Victoria', *Notes and Proceedings of the Legislative Council of Victoria*, II, A76.

Griffiths, T. 1987. *Beechworth: an Australian Country Town and its Past*, Melbourne.

Hall, A. R. 1963. 'Some long period effects of kinked age distribution of the population of Australia, 1861-1961', *Economic Record*, 39, March.

—— 1968. *The Stock Exchange of Melbourne, 1852-1900*, Canberra.

Hartz, L. 1964. *The Founding of New Societies*, New York.

Hirst, J. B. 1978. 'The pioneer legend', *Historical Studies*, 71, October.

Howe, R. 'The Wesleyan Church in Victoria 1855-1901: Its Ministry and Membership', M.A. Thesis, University of Melbourne.

Howitt, W. 1972. *Land, Labour and Gold*, Kilmore (1859).

Kelly, W. 1977. *Life in Victoria*, Kilmore (1859).

Kiddle, M. 1961. *Men of Yesterday*, Melbourne.

Lloyd, B. and Combes, H. 1981. *Gold at Gaffney's Creek*, Wangaratta.

Lloyd, B. 1982. *Gold at Harrietville*, Wangaratta.

—— 1978. *Gold at the Ten Mile*, Wangaratta.

McCarty, J. W. 1974. 'Australian Capital Cities in the Nineteenth Century', in C. B. Schedvin & J.W. McCarty (eds.), *Urbanization in Australia: The Nineteenth Century*, Sydney.

Martin, A. W. 1974. 'Australia and the Hartz "Fragment" Thesis', *Australian Economic History Review*, XIV (2).

Meredith, L. 1861. *Over The Straits: a Visit to Victoria*, London.

Molony, J. 1984. *Eureka*, Melbourne.

Morrell, W. P. 1940. *The Gold Rushes*, London.

Morrissey, J. J. 1966. 'The Character of Unassisted Immigration into

Victoria by Sea 1852-1860: a Study of Passenger Lists', B.A. Thesis (History), University of Melbourne.

Murray, R. and White, K. 1983. *The Golden Years of Stawell*, Melbourne.

O'Grady, D. 1985. *Raffaello! Raffaello!*, Sydney.

Nairn, B. 1973. *Civilizing Capitalism. The Labor Movement in New South Wales 1870-1900*, Canberra.

Palmer, Y. 1955. *Track of the Years. The Story of St. Arnaud*, Melbourne.

Potts, E. D. and A. (eds.) 1970. *A Yankee Merchant in Goldrush Australia*, Melbourne.

—— 1974. *Young America and Australian Gold*, St. Lucia, Brisbane.

Priestley, S. 1965. *Echuca*, Melbourne.

Richardson, H. H. 1930. *The Fortunes of Richard Mahony*, London.

Serle, G. 1954. 'The Causes of Eureka', *Historical Studies*, Eureka Supplement.

—— 1973. *From Deserts the Prophets Come: The Creative Spirit in Australia*, Melbourne.

—— 1963. *The Golden Age*, Melbourne.

—— 1970. 'The gold generation', *Victorian Historical Magazine*, 41 (1).

—— 1971. *The Rush to be Rich*, Melbourne.

Sinclair, W. A. 1976. *The Process of Economic Development in Australia*, Melbourne.

Smith, B. 1986. 'Two Art Systems', in *The Sydney Melbourne Book*, Melbourne.

Smyth, R. B. 1979. *The Goldfields and Mineral Districts of Victoria*, Melbourne (1860).

Stacpoole, H. J. 1971. *Gold at Ballarat*, Kilmore.

Trollope, A. 1873. *Australia and New Zealand*, Melbourne.

Ward, R. 1958. *The Australian Legend*, Melbourne.

Westgarth, W. 1857. *Victoria and the Australian Gold Mines in 1857*, London.

Williams, O. B. 1962. 'The Riverina and its Pastoral Industry 1860-1869' in A. Barnard (ed.), *The Simple Fleece*, Melbourne.

Withers, W. B. 1980. *A History of Ballarat*, Melbourne (1887).

Woods, C. 1985. *Beechworth: a Titan's Field*, Melbourne.

INDEX

agriculture, 18–19
  employment in, 38
Amalgamated Miners Association
  (A.M.A.), 48–9
  difference between Bendigo and
    Ballarat, 49
Americans, 26–8
  and Eureka, 43
  and transport, 21–2
  strong influence, 7, 41
Anderson Brothers, 13
army
  and Eureka, 43
  on goldfields, 41
art
  Heidelberg School, 64
  traditions in N.S.W. and Victoria,
    63
  see also Gill, S. T.
Australian Natives Association
  (A.N.A.), 47, 62

Bakery Hill, 42
Ballarat, 11, 13–14, 16–17, 23, 33,
  39–46
  changes in class structure, 31
  contrast with Bendigo, 14, 48–9
  federation enthusiasm, 62
  fine art gallery, 63

'Golden City' myth, 58
  Main Street, 52
  nature of the goldfield, 11, 42
  prelude to Eureka, 42
  South Street Society, 64
  unionism, 48–9
  urban growth, 52–4, 57
  workforce, 30
  weak local administration, 43
Ballarat Bank, 13
Ballarat Reform League, 41, 44
Bathurst, 21
Beaufort, 39
Beechworth, 11, 14
Bendigo, 11, 13–14, 17, 23, 33, 39
  class structure, 30
  contrast with Ballarat, 14, 48–9
  ethnic concentrations, 28
  federation enthusiasm, 62
  friendly societies, 47
  Germans in quartz mining, 28
  social character, 36
  town centre, 58
  unionism, 48–9
  unrest in 1853–4, 42–3
  urban growth, 52–4
benevolent institutions, 32
Bentley, James, 43
Blainey, G. N., 4, 6, 42–6

73

home ownership, 30–31
horses, 20–21
hotels, 38–9
  Bentley's Eureka Hotel, 43
  burning of Bentley's hotel, 43–4
Hotham, Sir Charles, 27, 42–5
  and Eureka, 42–5
Howitt, William, 34

imports from Britain, 4, 15–16
  from America, 7, 16
industry, 9, 17–19, 53–5
investment; *see* capital, economy
Irish, 27–8
  at Eureka, 43–5
  favoured by rough conditions, 28

Jews, 27

Kelly, William, 35
Kiandra, 11, 33

Labor Party, 48, 50, 61
labour intensive activities, 20
labour shortages, 8
law and order, 41, 44
Lawson, Henry, 64–5
leasehold, 14
Legislative Council, 6
  barrier to change, 40, 46
  composition, 41
Leviathan coach, 21
Liberal political organization, 61
licence hunt, 41–2, 45
Lindsay family, 63
literature, 34–5, 64
  different traditions in N.S.W. and
    Victoria, 64
local financial systems
  on goldfields, 12
local government, 40, 45
location of Victorian gold towns,
  1871, 55

McNaughton, I. D.
  views about relative importance of
    gold rush, 59–61
manufacturing; *see* industry
Martin, A. W.

on cultural transmission, criticism
  of Hartz's views, 25
masculinity, 29, 34–5, 37–8, 40
materialism, 39–40
mateship, 35–6, 50, 65
Melbourne
  art tradition, 63–4
  boom during 1880s, 24, 29
  investment centre, 14, 24
  local government, 40
  'Marvellous Melbourne', 40, 58,
    65
  metropolitan status, 58
  migrant centre, 32
  population, 24, 29, 51–2
  supply centre, 24
Meredith, Louisa, 52
metal industry, 17–18, 53–5, 57
Methodists, 46–7
Michie, A.
  comment on quality of migrants,
    30
middle class and art, 64
migration
  arrivals and departures, 27
  characteristics of migrants, 28–30,
    35
  contrast between pastoral and
    goldrush migrants, 26
  ethnic mix of migrants, 26–7
  family reunion, 29
  influx of women, 29, 36
  links with Britain, 26
  nature of migrant societies, 25
  pressure from, in 1857, 16
  radical elements in, 26
  Victorian population structure, 33
Miner's Right
  housing and social stability, 40
mining investment; *see* capital,
  economy
mining, pastoralism and agriculture
  compared, 9
Montez, Lola, 39
moralizing, 32, 39
Mount Alexander (Castlemaine), 32
mutual improvement societies, 47

natural protection, 17, 19, 21, 54

76